Do Bees Sneeze?

And Other Questions Kids Ask About Insects

James K. Wangberg

fulcrum resources

Fulcrum Publishing
Golden, Colorado

To Lesley, Stephanie, and Ryan

Text copyright © 1997 by James K. Wangberg
Cover illustration © 1997 by Anna-Maria Crum
Illustrations copyright © 1997 by Ellen Parker
Illustrations for chapter openers
   copyright © 1997 by James K. Wangberg

Book design by Deborah Rich
Cover design by Bill Spahr

Library of Congress Cataloging-in-Publication Data

Wangberg, James K. (James Keith)
   Do bees sneeze? : and other questions kids ask about insects / James K. Wangberg ; illustrated by Ellen Parker.
       p.   cm.
   Includes bibliographical references and index.
   Summary: Questions and answers explore the insect world, in such categories as body parts and functions, behavior, and habitats.
   ISBN 1-55591-963-4 (pbk.)
   1. Insects—Miscellanea—Juvenile literature. [1. Insects—Miscellanea. 2. Questions and answers.] I. Parker, Ellen (Ellen J.), ill. II. Title.
QL467.2.W36   1997
595.7—dc21   97-6057
                                                          CIP
                                                           AC

Printed in the United States of America
0 9 8 7 6 5 4 3 2 1

Fulcrum Publishing
350 Indiana Street, Suite 350
Golden, Colorado 80401-5093
(800) 992-2908 • (303) 277-1623

Contents

3

Body Parts & Functions   41

Do Bees Sneeze?

4

Size, Strength, & Speed   79

5

Behavior   89

Do Bees Sneeze?

6

Homes & Habitats   119

7 Foods for Insects & Insects as Food   147

Do Bees Sneeze?

8

Health & Safety   163

9

Insect Relatives   173

ix

Contents

x

Do Bees Sneeze?

Acknowledgments

I am extremely grateful to all the children, teachers, and parents who helped generate and submit questions, thus making this book possible. Thanks to their schools for supporting their educational endeavors.

Several entomologist colleagues assisted by verifying facts, providing additional information, and suggesting answers: James Cochendolpher, John George, Phil Kaufman, Jack Lloyd, Jeffrey Lockwood, David Richman, William A. Shear, and Scott Shaw.

Special thanks go to Richard Hurley and Darryl Sanders for reviewing the manuscript and for their helpful additions to the text. I am grateful to Whitney Cranshaw for directing me to Fulcrum Publishing and extend a special thank you to Suzanne Barchers of Fulcrum for her professional and enthusiastic support.

My secretary, Amy Slack, deserves countless credit for a variety of help and clerical tasks, and Chanin Gates is gratefully acknowledged for helping both of us.

My good friend, and the book's illustrator, Ellen Parker, is appreciated not only for her fine drawings but also for her insights and counsel throughout the project.

Thanks to Sandra Guzzo for her advice to a first-time book author.

I am also indebted to *Learning* Magazine for advertising the book writing project, which attracted questions from kids throughout the United States.

The University of Wyoming deserves credit for providing the setting, resources, and professional atmosphere for such an undertaking and for annual support of educational outreach throughout the state and region.

Lastly, I give special thanks and acknowledgments to my wife and children for the joy they bring to my life each and every day.

Introduction

An added pleasure in my 20-plus-year career as a professor of entomology has been the opportunity to visit children of all ages at schools, libraries, museums, clubs, and special educational events to talk about the fascinating world of insects. Although I am generally accustomed to the types of questions posed by my college students, I have continually been surprised, amused, and impressed with the questions that come from youngsters. The questions kids ask about bugs, although at a different intellectual level from those of an adult student, nonetheless reflect the perspective and joy that only naive and curious young people possess. Few adults would ask, "Does an insect sneeze?" but what a wonderful question and entrée into the intriguing lives of insects. Questions like this, from children around the country, were the inspiration for this book.

This book is written for children of all ages and for the teachers, librarians, museum staff, educational program leaders, parents, and other adults who, like me, are faced with a myriad of questions from kids about bugs. The questions were obtained during visits to schools and through personal contacts and published solicitation. The child who asked each question is identified by first name and/or grade level, school, city, and state. The questions selected for the book were among the most commonly asked or ones that I considered to be of greatest interest. One question was often asked by more than one child, in which case I tried to balance the number of schools and locales represented. There are 210 questions from children representing 18 schools or home schools, 16 cities, and 13 states from Maine to California and Minnesota to Texas. Many more questions were not included because of space constraints.

How to Use the Book

Questions are grouped by common themes in nine chapters: Abundance and Existence, Appearance, Body Parts and Functions, and so on. Each question is written as the child posed it, with a few exceptions for grammar, and answered with a minimum of technical jargon and scientific terminology. Within each chapter, related questions follow each other. At the end of each chapter are proposed projects and activities related to the chapter theme that children, with adult supervision, can undertake for exploring the biology and behavior of insects and their relatives.

This book can be a quick and easy reference for answering children's questions; simply refer to the appropriate chapter and seek the question within the table of contents. Chances are good that most questions posed will be answered in the book. If not, there is likely a similar question and answer for comparison.

This book can supplement existing curricula or be a periodic guide to special activities. Questions from the book can be posed to quiz students and pique curiosity and to stimulate the generation of additional questions about bugs. The book can be a useful guide or supplement for student research and projects. The proposed projects at the end of each chapter can serve as special activities and be modified or expanded to meet student or class needs and interests. The references cited will assist in obtaining additional information.

As with all endeavors that involve finding answers to questions, the use of this book may very well generate more questions, which, after all, is the essence and joy of science—the continual exploration and discovery of new things and new challenges.

Enjoy the world of entomology with this book and a child!

Please note: The names of common insects in this book are spelled correctly according to the Entomological Society of America's standing Committee on Common Names of Insects, but the spelling may disagree with that listed in your dictionary. Some insects' names in this book are spelled with two words because they are true flies, bugs, and so on (house fly and stink bug), while others are not true flies and bugs (butterfly and tumblebug). Since I am explaining some of the true entomological natures of insects, I think it is only right to include the true entomological spellings.

1 Abundance & Existence

TICK NEEDS a RIDE with good host

How many insects are there in the whole world?

Get ready for some astronomical figures! An insect population count or insect census can be only a guess because it is impossible to count them all. Some people believe there are nearly a quintillion (1,000,000,000,000,000,000) insects in the world! That is 200 million times greater than the nearly five billion people that live on earth. For every person on the planet, there are more than 200 million insects! (Wigglesworth 1964, 13).

Jamin, combined 3rd and 4th grades
Hutton Elementary School
Spokane, Washington

2 How many different kinds of bugs are there?

About one million species (or kinds) of insects have been named, and we think at least that many more remain to be discovered. Some people believe there are over 10 million species. New species are being discovered every day!

4th grader
Pleasanton Elementary School
Pleasanton, Texas

3 Will insects overpopulate the world?

You might think that with more than one million species and a population of nearly a quintillion that the world is already overpopulated with insects, but it is not. It is not likely to become overpopulated, at least not for very long, because nature has its own checks and balances. If any living thing becomes overabundant, then such things as starvation, disease, killings, and loss of space and shelter cause deaths and result in lower populations. In the insect world it is not uncommon to see population explosions that last for months or a few years such as the great locust plagues that occur in Africa, but nature eventually causes the numbers to come crashing down, and the overpopulation problem ends.

Adam, combined 3rd and 4th grades
Hutton Elementary School
Spokane, Washington

4 Why do insects exist?

Insects exist because they have so many marvelous ways to live in different places and habitats around the world. They have body structures and functions that give them special advantages over other animals, and they possess the size, strength, and speed necessary to be

Do Bees Sneeze?

successful. Insects behave in a fantastic number of ways that also give them advantages in their environment and against enemies and competitors. They reproduce rapidly and in large numbers so that there are always many chances for their survival. These and many other things about their biology are the reasons insects exist.

> Insects feed on virtually all kinds of plant and animal foods and have developed special ways to obtain the nutrition they need to live and reproduce.

Joseph, 5th grade
Starpoint Intermediate
Lockport, New York

5 Are there any extinct bugs?

Absolutely. There are many kinds of fossil insects that no longer exist today. We really don't know how many total insects may have become extinct, but the number is probably big. Some entomologists have estimated that 20–30 insect species become extinct every day—or about one insect extinction every hour! The insects in the greatest danger live in endangered habitats or in very special and fragile places. The tropical rain forests, for example, are being threatened in certain parts of the world, and as those forests disappear so do the insects that depend on them for shelter and food. If we damage our environments, then we risk damaging the insects and other living things that are found there.

Ana, 7th grade
Wyoming Center for Teaching and Learning
Laramie, Wyoming

6 What was the first bug on Earth?

No one knows what the first insect on Earth was because the oldest insect fossils include many different kinds, many of which resemble insects of today. The

3

Abundance & Existence

oldest known six-legged insectlike creature, called a springtail, existed 350 million years ago. The first true insect was probably a small, wingless type that resembles a modern-day silverfish (Evans 1984, 36).

Ana, 7th grade
Wyoming Center for Teaching and Learning
Laramie, Wyoming

7 How long have insects been alive?

All of the major groups of insects that exist today, including fleas, lice, ants, bees, wasps, butterflies and moths, and plant hoppers, are believed to have been alive by the Cenozoic era, about 35 million years ago. Many insects have existed even longer. In the Jurassic period, or age of the dinosaurs (180 million years ago), there were already mayflies, dragonflies and damselflies, roaches, grasshoppers and crickets, true bugs, beetles, caddisflies, flies, and others (Evans 1984, 44).

The common silverfish

Kelly, combined 3rd and 4th grades
Hutton Elementary School
Spokane, Washington

8 How many different kinds of butterflies and moths are there in the whole world?

There are more than 110,000 species or different kinds of butterflies and moths in the world. They are the third most abundant group of insects, after beetles and flies

(300,000) and midges, gnats, and mosquitoes (120,000) (Borror, Triplehorn, and Johnson 1989, 147).

Erin, 6th grade
Wyoming Center for Teaching and Learning
Laramie, Wyoming

9

How many ants are there in the whole world?
There are about a quadrillion (1,000,000,000,000,000), or a thousand trillion, ants living on the earth at any given moment. That's one-tenth of 1 percent of the estimated total population of insects on earth (Wilson 1971, 27–28).

Nicholas, 5th grade
Starpoint Intermediate
Lockport, New York

10

How many ants are in a colony?
It depends on the type of ant. Some ants that are thought to be primitive, or old-fashioned, have colonies of just a few individuals. Some ant colonies, like leaf cutters, harvester ants, and army ants, number in the tens of thousands.

Ana, 7th grade
Wyoming Center for Teaching and Learning
Laramie, Wyoming

11

What is the most recent insect discovered?
Insects are being discovered, described, and named all the time. While I write this answer, another entomologist somewhere is discovering a new insect species and getting excited about telling other scientists.

Drew, 3rd grade
Manor Heights Elementary School
Casper, Wyoming

5

Abundance & Existence

12

What is the most common insect seen in the United States?

That's difficult to answer because some insects are very common in some parts of the country and rare or not existent in other parts of the country. My guess would be that, in general, ants of one type or another are the most commonly seen insects in the United States. Ants are numerous (see question 9) and live throughout the country. Even people who do not know much about insects usually recognize an ant when they see one. As far as a certain species of insect goes, I would guess that the house fly or honey bee is the most commonly seen insect, or at least the most commonly seen and recognized. The house fly is noticed a lot as a nuisance around our homes, and the honey bee is often seen in gardens and fields visiting flowers. There are many other insects that are probably seen as much or more than these two, but people may not know their names.

Heather, 5th grade
Starpoint Intermediate
Lockport, New York

13

What is the most uncommon insect seen in the United States?

Whew! That is even tougher to answer. Let's ignore those insects that don't naturally occur in the United States but may sometimes get here by accident. Considering the insects that normally live in the United States, I would say that a group of insects called zorapterans (they don't have a more common name) are the most uncommon. There are only about 30 kinds of zorapterans known in the world, and only three kinds live in the United States. They are very small, about 3 millimeters or less in length, and they like to hide in sawdust piles or under tree bark or live with termites. I would guess

Do Bees Sneeze?

that most entomologists have never seen a live zorapteran. Only the scientists with special interests in this group are likely to encounter or notice them (Borror, Triplehorn, and Johnson 1989, 258).

Heather, 5th grade
Starpoint Intermediate
Lockport, New York

The uncommon zorapteran

7

Abundance & Existence

Making Your Own Ant Farm

Many people are familiar with ant farms that can be purchased, but this activity project will tell you how to build your own. It's easy, and the homemade ant farm may actually be better than what you can buy.

Materials Needed

- two widemouthed glass or transparent plastic jars, one larger than the other so the small jar can be placed inside the large jar. Use jars of about the same height and select a smaller jar that is not too much smaller than the large one.
- clean, fine-textured soil or sand-soil mix (best if collected from area where ants are collected)
- some string or sticks
- a small sponge, or cotton balls, or any other absorbent material
- ants!

Build the Farm

To build your ant farm, simply place the small jar inside the large one and pour a soil or soil-sand mixture in the narrow space between the two jars. Do not put soil inside the small jar. Place a wet sponge or other absorbent material in the small jar as a water source for the ants and place two or three strings or sticks to serve as ant ladders from the soil between the two jars to the bottom of the small jar where the sponge is located. Collect a large number of ants from a nest in the soil and place them in the portion of the jar containing the soil. Place a tight-fitting lid or cover on the jar to prevent escapes, but make tiny air holes in it so that the ants can breathe. Cover the jar with a paper wrap or place in a dark closet or drawer and let the ants settle down undisturbed in their new home. After one or two days you may examine them and begin to feed them and observe their activities.

Observing the Ants

They should make rapid progress in constructing their new nest, and you can observe them as they build tunnels, communicate with each other, and handle their daily chores. If you know what kind of food your ants prefer, place small amounts of it in the bottom of the small jar. If you are not sure what to feed your ants, then experiment by offering small amounts of dead insects or your own food scraps. Observing your ants' behavior in nature before collecting them will help you understand their food habits. The ants will quickly learn that their food and water are located on the other side of their ladders, and you will see them traveling back and forth. You may also discover that they will turn some of their area into a cemetery where dead ants will be piled.

Your homemade ant farm is ideal because you can view the colony from any point around the jar and easily tend to water and food supplies without disturbing the actual ant nest that is constructed in the soil area. Unless you are lucky enough to have captured a queen, your ant farm may last for only several weeks or a few months, but it will still provide hours of fascinating ant behavior observations and opportunities to experiment. You could make several ant farms of the same or different kinds of ants and have the ant ladders go to some shared watering and feeding grounds. What will ants from different colonies do when they find themselves competing for food or water?

When you have finished observing and experimenting with your ants, return them to their original home.

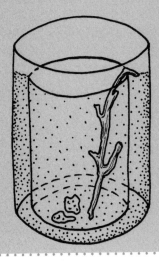

An easily homemade ant farm

Making Collecting Equipment

One of the nice things about insect collecting is that it doesn't require a lot of fancy equipment. There are two basic collecting tools: a net and a kill jar. Each can be purchased from biological supply dealers, but here are some tips for making your own.

Making an Insect Net

You will need a long handle, like a broom handle; some light net or mesh fabric (panty hose works well) or muslin cloth, depending upon how rough the vegetation is where the net will be used or if you wish to easily see what is captured (a loose weave mesh is best); and a wire or coat hanger for the net hoop. Sew the net bag in the shape of a wind sock with a diameter of 10 to 12 inches and a depth of about 18 inches. The size of the net really depends upon your personal preference. Stitch along the margin of the net's open mouth to create a sleeve for the metal hoop. Shape a stout wire or coat hanger to the proper diameter circle and run it through the stitched margin. There should be several inches of protruding wire that can be wrapped around and taped securely to the handle, or preferably, inserted into drilled holes and bent around the handle and then taped to anchor it securely.

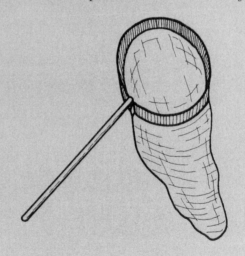

A standard insect net

Do Bees Sneeze?

Selecting a Kill Jar

There are different types of kill jars—the best are dry containers that kill insects through fumigation. The alternative is to collect and kill insects by placing them in alcohol. This method works well for immature and soft-bodied insects but not for adults and winged insects. You must determine the level of safety needed for the age group that will use the killing apparatus before deciding on what type to construct. Insect kill jars contain poisons. Professional entomologists may use cyanide, an extremely hazardous and deadly compound that should not be used by the amateur. The safest killing agent may be rubbing alcohol, but it is not the most efficient in overpowering larger insects; even rubbing alcohol may be hazardous if misused or abused. Ethyl acetate, or the solvent used in fingernail polish remover, is a better agent against insects, but the fumes are more hazardous and its use should be carefully supervised as well. If the use of poisons is not an option, then consider collecting insects in a jar and killing them by placing the jar in a freezer. Freezing is a humane, effective, and safe method for the younger collector.

Making a Kill Jar

To build a dry kill jar for fumigating insects, select a widemouthed jar with a tight-fitting lid. A peanut butter jar will work, and the jar should be wide and shallow enough to permit easy reach with the hand or fingers. Glass jars are perfect except for the inherent breakage hazard. Plastic jars are good unless you intend to use ethyl acetate, which can dissolve certain plastics. In the bottom of the jar place an inch or two of absorbent material (cotton, sawdust, paper), and on top of that place a precut, snugly fitting floor of cardboard to separate the insects from the moisture. Add the selected poison (rubbing alcohol, ethyl

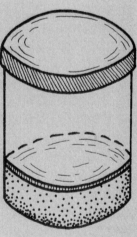

A standard insect killing jar

acetate) to the absorbent material, soaking it thoroughly but not leaving excess floating above the cardboard floor. The jar is now charged and ready to use. As an added safety measure, wrap the bottom part of the jar with duct tape so, in the event the jar breaks, glass and poison will not be injected into the skin.

Using a Kill Jar

Insects placed in a freshly charged jar will be knocked down by the fumes and will die after several minutes of exposure. Leave the insects in the jar for an ample time to ensure death. It is not pleasant to see insects come back to life after they have been pinned and put in a collection! If insects struggle a lot and die slowly, add more poison to the jar. The more the jar is opened and used, the more often it will have to be recharged. Always open the jar outdoors or in well-ventilated areas, and never hold it close to your face where fumes could be inhaled. Treat a kill jar with respect and be a safe collector.

Do Bees Sneeze?

Making a Collection

It is easy to make an insect collection because most of the materials that you need can be found in the home or can be easily purchased. In addition, most insects do not require any preservatives or special techniques to make them last. The collected insects need only be pinned and allowed to dry in a covered box.

Preserving Insects

Adult insects that have been collected and killed (see Making Collecting Equipment) should be placed on a pin as soon as possible, before the body gets dry and brittle. Caterpillars and other immature or soft-bodied insects are preserved in alcohol and not pinned. Only butterflies and dragonflies should have their wings spread and dried (an explanation for spreading butterfly wings follows). Most insects are ready to be permanently pinned as soon as they have died. Wings, legs, and antennae do not have to be positioned in any particular manner.

Pinning Insects

To pin insects, it is best to use professional insect pins available from biological supply companies because the pins are sized differently for different insects and are more attractive, but straight pins will work if you can't obtain insect pins. The placement of the pin is important and depends on the type of insect being pinned. All insects are pinned in the thorax. Most are pinned to the right of center and about midway along the thorax length. Only butterflies and moths should be pinned directly in the center of the thorax. True bugs get pinned in the upper right "shoulder," as do grasshoppers. The insect should be positioned near the top of the pin so that 1/2 of an inch of

A properly pinned
and labeled insect

13

the pin protrudes above the insect and serves as a convenient handle. Try to place the pin as straight up and down as possible.

Labeling Insects

The serious collector or student should make a label to accompany each insect on its pin. A label made of unlined cardstock, no larger than 1/4 by 3/4 inches, should have the following information legibly printed in ink upon it:

- where insect was collected: 2 mi. E. Laramie, Albany Co., WY
- date collected: IX-6-97 (month in Roman numerals)
- name of collector: J. Wangberg

An optional and separate label for the name of the insect can be included if desired. Any and all abbreviations can be used because space is limited on the label. The label is pinned and aligned with the insect's body so that specimen and label occupy a minimum of space.

Where to Keep Your Insect Collection

Once the insect is properly pinned, place it in any box of adequate depth that has a securely fitting lid and a porous floor to easily receive and secure the pinned specimens. A cigar box or shoebox with a corrugated cardboard or cork floor will work fine. Styrofoam items, such as meat trays from grocery stores, work very well. Arrange the insects neatly and in whatever manner suits you. Uniformity and efficient use of space make for the most attractive collections.

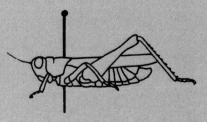
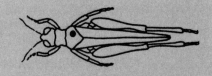

Proper pinning technique for insects

Do Bees Sneeze?

Protecting Your Insect Collection

To protect your pinned specimens from tiny insects that easily find and invade insect collections, sprinkle some moth crystals in the box and replenish them regularly. A lot of effort at collecting and preserving insects can be destroyed in a few months by other insect invaders. To preserve the colors of butterflies and moths it is wise to keep the collection covered and out of direct light.

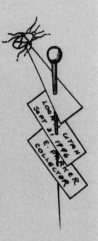

Mounting Butterflies

Now, back to the special spreading and pinning technique for those beautiful butterflies. Butterfly wings should be spread when still fresh so the front and hind wings can be seen fully. Use a

Tiny insects can be glued to paper "points" for proper pinning and labeling.

spreading board or a styrofoam sheet to position the insect. Working one side at a time, gently slide the front wing forward until its hind edge is perpendicular to the thorax. Hold it in place with a pinned strip of paper and then slide the hind wing forward so that its front edge is overlapped just slightly by the front wing. Once both are properly positioned, hold them firmly in place with pinned paper strips. Repeat the procedure for the other wings. Allow several days for wings to dry (the larger the insect, the greater the drying time). When you think the insect has stiffened, remove one pin at a time, and if wings don't move, then all is well and the butterfly is ready to be placed in the collection.

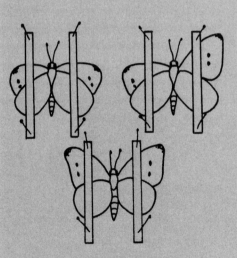

Steps and technique for spreading butterfly wings

Night-Light Insect Collecting

Many insects are attracted to lights, which creates some excellent opportunities to observe or collect them.

Collecting in the Dark

The simplest technique is to place a sheet or other large white fabric behind a porch light. If it's not convenient to use a porch light, any other bright source of light (lantern, high-beam flashlight, spotlight) with a white sheet behind it will work well. Entomologists use what's called a blacklight, because it gives off a type of light called ultraviolet light that is particularly attractive to insects, but any bright light will attract some insects. If your light source is a mobile one, then try to set up your light and sheet in what you think might be a rich insect habitat, such as on the edge of a pond, lake, or stream, on the edge of a wooded area, or in an open field or pasture. Parking a vehicle in such an area and placing a sheet over the windshield with a light powered from the vehicle's accessory outlets is a great way to collect.

Soon after dark, insects will fly to the light and collect all over the sheet. Many will fly about and others will scamper around the light on the sheet. See how many different kinds of insects come to the light. How many can you identify? Where do you think they came from? Do the insects that come to the light pay any attention to each other? (Hint: some may come to the light and actually feast on the others!) Insects are easily collected with fingers, forceps, or with the aid of a jar. Warm summer nights are the best time to collect, and after a recent rain there are often huge insect flights.

Setting up a Permanent Night Trap

If you wish to set up a permanent nighttime insect-collecting station, then consider a screened booth with a light on top and a funnel beneath the light to channel insects into the screened booth. In this way you can leave a light on all night and come back in the morning to observe a full night's capture or remain by the booth and enter at will to collect the insects you want.

Do Bees Sneeze?

Constructing Berlese Funnels

Millions of insects live at or beneath the soil surface in the rich layers of humus and leaf litter. Most go unnoticed for their entire lives because of their secretive habits and small size. It is not practical to try and collect them with insect nets and other conventional equipment, and it is too time consuming to sift or sort through soil by hand in search of minute insects. A device that you can build, called a Berlese funnel, is an efficient way to find, collect, and study the hidden world of soil and litter insects.

Materials Needed
- a 1- or 2-gallon plastic or metal bucket
- about 1 square foot of 1/4-inch mesh screen
- a gooseneck or adjustable lamp with 100-watt bulb
- a funnel with the same diameter as the bucket (you can simply make one of cardboard)
- duct tape
- a peanut butter jar
- rubbing alcohol

Building a Berlese Funnel
First, cut out the bottom of the bucket to create a cylinder. Shape a funnel out of some cardboard or other flexible but sturdy material so that the wide end is the same diameter as the cylinder, and tape it to the bottom. Cut a circular piece of 1/4-inch mesh screen slightly smaller than the funnel diameter and place it to fit securely near the top of the funnel. Support the funnel with a stand or some sturdy props so that it stands upright, with the narrow tip suspended above a jar filled about halfway with alcohol. Position a lamp with 100-watt bulb above the upper, open end of the cylinder. You are now ready to collect insects that hide in litter and humus.

Collecting with the Berlese Funnel
Find an area where the soil is covered with a rich and moist layer of leaf litter or other natural debris. Do not gather dry material

and do not gather clean, inorganic soil. Gather enough natural debris in a paper bag to nearly fill the cylinder that you have constructed. Place the litter sample in the Berlese funnel, atop the screen (you should remove the alcohol jar when filling the funnel to avoid the mess of extra debris falling through). Once the litter is contained in the funnel, reposition the jar under the funnel and move the lighted lamp back over the top. Do not put the lamp so close as to create a fire hazard, but put it close enough so the heat from the bulb will gradually dry out the moist sample. Leave the lamp in place for 24 hours. As the light dries out the litter, the insects that were collected with it will move downward, away from the heat and toward the receding band of moisture. Eventually, they will travel to the funnel tip and drop into the alcohol. After 24 hours you can turn off the light and examine the jar's contents. You will be amazed at the number and diversity of soil arthropods that have been collected from just a small litter sample. You will need a magnifying lens or low-power microscope to see most of them. A field guide can help in identifying them.

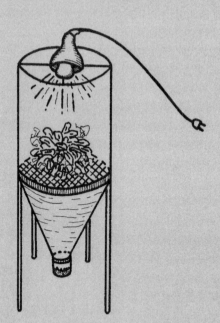

The Berlese funnel is a good device for collecting the tiny insects that live and hide in leaf litter.

Making one Berlese funnel collection can be an interesting adventure, but it is also interesting to gather different kinds of litter from different areas to compare the various insects and other arthropods. The collection is always a surprise, because you won't see the creatures in the litter while you are gathering it. They will only make themselves known by falling into the jar of alcohol.

Do Bees Sneeze?

Arranging an Insect Scavenger Hunt

An insect scavenger hunt is a fun activity for exploring insect habitats, observing insect behaviors, and testing collecting skills. You can design a scavenger hunt to emphasize a theme or involve certain activities, or it can be very general in nature. Ideally, a scavenger hunt will occur outdoors at a time of year when insects are plentiful, but if you are limited by season or access to natural environments you can be creative and design an indoor scavenger hunt and utilize insect collections, living insects in the classroom, and the photographs of insects in books, other literature, or on the computer. Designing the scavenger hunt list can be as much fun as the hunt itself. The hunt can be a cooperative activity, a competitive activity or game, or an individual project.

Here is a scavenger hunt list that we have used in an "Insects for Teachers" class at the University of Wyoming as an example of what can be developed:

- an insect that feeds on pollen
- an insect that feeds on nectar
- a stem or root where an insect has tunneled
- an insect gall
- a dung insect
- an insect parasite
- an insect that lives underground
- an insect that hides under ground cover
- an insect that lives its entire life in water
- an insect that lives part of its life in water
- an insect that lives on the water surface
- an insect that lives under water in the mud
- an insect with a beak
- an insect with biting-chewing jaws

- an insect predator
- an insect that feeds on plants
- an insect with jumping legs
- an insect with swimming legs
- an insect with digging legs
- an insect with grasping legs
- an insect egg
- an insect larva
- an insect pupa or cocoon
- a social insect
- an insect that sings
- an insect with warning colors
- an insect mimic (i.e., a fly that looks like a bee)
- the old, cast-off skin of an insect
- an insect nest
- an insect with camouflage
- an insect with eyespots

Do Bees Sneeze?

2 Appearance

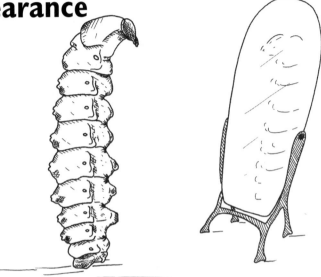

Mirror, mirror on the wall,
who's the fairest grub of all?

Are there some insects that you can't see?

Some insects are extremely difficult for people to see because of their tiny size or disguises. Also, most insect eggs are quite small. You may not be happy to learn that much of the food we eat has tiny insects and insect eggs in it and we eat them without ever realizing it. The smallest insect adult is the fairyfly (see question 1, Chapter 4), but there is another small insect that is so difficult to see that it has been named the no-see-um! The no-see-um is a tiny biting midge that likes to bite people and animals. You will feel them biting around your neck, ears, and face, but you will not see them. They seem to be invisible.

Dreshard, combined 3rd and 4th grades
Hutton Elementary School
Spokane, Washington

A lot of insects are big enough to see, but they have excellent disguises that make them difficult to spot. The walkingstick is one of the most famous. Its sticklike body, legs, color, and texture look so much like a stick that only close examination or its movement will give it away. Praying mantids, katydids, and grasshoppers may be perfect copies of green or brown leaves and flowers and go undiscovered. Some insects are colored and patterned to match the soil and rocks where they live. Some plant hoppers look like rose thorns, and some insects called scales look like spots or scabs on a plant and not like a living thing. They are easily seen but oftentimes not recognized to be insects.

2 How many colors can insects be?

Insects can be almost any color. Insect colors may be drab and dull or bright and beautiful. Insects can be white, black, yellow, green, red, orange, brown, purple, blue, gray, and any mixture of colors, just like the colors you can make when you mix paints together. Some insects may have just one color or appear to be a solid color, and others may have multiple colors and markings. The colors insects have may help them hide, warn their enemies, signal mates or members of a colony, or help confuse their enemies.

Victoria, 5th grade
Starpoint Intermediate
Lockport, New York

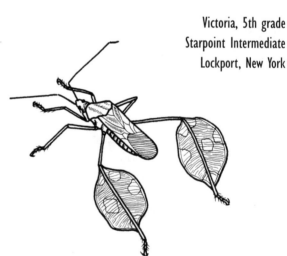

The leaf footed bug has legs disguised as leaves. From the tip of its head to the end of its body measures about one inch.

Do Bees Sneeze?

3 What is the most colorful bug?

There are so many colorful insects that it is not easy to say which is the most colorful. Some of the most colorful are the insects with bright, metallic colors. There are some beetles, called metallic wood borers, that can be beautifully colored—bronze, copper, metallic green, blue, or purple. There are some other beetles called scarabs that may be so colorful that they look like jewels. Some moths from Madagascar, called sunset moths, have a spectacular, rich mixture of colors. The morpho, a tropical butterfly, has wings that are iridescent blue on top but drab brown on the undersides. The butterflies and moths known as Lepidoptera (lep-ah-dop-tir-ah) are often recognized as being the most colorful.

Supreet, 2nd grade
Charles Quentin Elementary School
Lake Zurich, Illinois

4 How do butterflies get their pretty colors?

Butterflies get their beautiful colors in two ways. Some colors come from chemicals called pigments, and some colors appear because of special structures on the insect that reflect light in special ways. Here is an explanation. When you see colors like white, yellow, orange, red, brown, and black on butterflies it is because they have pigments to

> The scales or flattened hairs that cover butterfly wings will often reflect sunlight in ways that produce these beautiful colors. Just as the colors of the rainbow are due to light being broken up, the colors of many insects are caused by light being broken up by insect structures, like the scales on insect wings.

give them those colors. Our skin can be different colors because of different skin pigments, just as our eyes may be of different colors because of eye pigments. Insects have pigments too.

23

Appearance

But when you see metallic colors, colors that seem shiny or iridescent, and colors that glisten in the sun sometimes changing with the angle of sunlight, then you are seeing colors caused by insect structures, not by insect pigments.

3rd and 4th graders
Hutton Elementary School
Spokane, Washington

5 What is the purpose of colors in a brightly colored bug?

Bright colors in insects can have many purposes. Some bright colors serve as warning colors (see question 9). If an insect is brightly colored, especially with red and black, yellow and black, or orange and black, then it may mean "beware, I can sting, I can bite, I taste bad, I smell bad, or there is something nasty about me that you will not like—stay away!"

The monarch butterfly is a bright orange and black insect that has a poison in its body. If a bird eats the monarch it will get very sick to its stomach and remember not to mess with monarchs again. Sometimes, however, these brightly colored insects are copycats and have warning colors like stinging, biting, or bad-tasting insects, but they do not have any kind of defense. They may fool their enemies by looking dangerous when they are actually quite harmless. They are called insect mimics. Sometimes bright colors help insects find and recognize their mates. Many male butterflies are more brightly colored than the females, just like many birds, and this is a way they can recognize each other.

Some insects use colors and color patterns as signals. There are some flies, called picture-winged flies, that have colored markings on their wings, which they display during fancy courtship dances. The males strut about like peacocks trying to attract the female's attention. Some insects are brightly colored to blend in with brightly colored flowers where they live. One magnificent

Do Bees Sneeze?

insect, the flower mantid, is a praying mantid that looks just like a bright pink orchid, and this allows it to hide from its enemies and sneak up on unsuspecting prey.

6th-grade class
Thayer Elementary School
Laramie, Wyoming

6 Do insect eggs come in colors or plain white?

Many insect eggs are white or light colored, but there are also many examples of colored insect eggs. There are bright red, yellow, and orange eggs; dark brown and black eggs; and eggs that have more than one color, some striped or with colored bands. Insect eggs can come in almost the same variety of colors as insect adults.

4th grader
Anthony T. Lane Elementary School
Alexandria, Virginia

7 How do insects change color?

A few insects can change colors to match their surroundings but not as easily as a chameleon can. A praying mantid, for example, may be green when resting among green leaves, but if it moves to a background of dead leaves and branches it will gradually darken to tan or brown and remain nicely hidden. It does this by special chemical changes in its body. Most insects that are well camouflaged are born that way and have the colors, shapes, and markings that are best suited for their special habitats.

Brittany, 2nd grade
Linford Elementary School
Laramie, Wyoming

8 What colors are cocoons?

Insect cocoons are made of silk, and some insects will add materials like leaves and sticks to their cocoons.

25

Appearance

The color depends on the nature of the silk and the extra materials that are used. Insect silk and silken cocoons can be white to dirty white, gray, or brownish in color. Some may start out bright white but end up drab gray because of the soil and debris surrounding them. Some insect cocoons may be multicolored, like those of a tiny wasp that emerges from a white cocoon that has a black band around it.

> Some cocoons are very thin and you can see through them. These cocoons don't have much color, but the color of the insect inside can be seen.

Jason, combined 3rd and 4th grades
Hutton Elementary School
Spokane, Washington

9 Why are bees black and yellow?

Many bees and wasps are black and yellow to warn others that they can sting. These insects have what are called warning colors so that other animals will quickly learn to leave them alone; they are nature's stop signs. We learn at a very young age that stop signs are red, that a red traffic light means stop, and that a lot of other warnings come in red. In the same way, the natural enemies of insects have learned to recognize red and black, orange and black, and yellow and black as signs of danger. When all bees use the same or similar colors and markings as their warning devices, they are easier to remember.

Dan, 2nd grade
Greenvale Park School
Northfield, Minnesota

10 Why are some mealworms white and some yellow?

It is not unusual to find white or very pale mealworms among the normal yellowish or tan mealworms. Many

Do Bees Sneeze?

people mistake these for albino mealworms, or mealworms without body color. They are not albinos but rather
mealworms that are busy molting or shedding their skin.
Mealworms, like all young, growing insects, must shed
their skins once in a while in order to grow larger. After
they shed the skin they have outgrown, just as we give
away clothes that no longer fit, the mealworms are soft
and pale as they wait for their new, larger skin to grow
and harden. It may take less than an hour for mealworms
to get hard and have their color return, but during that
brief time they stand out from the rest because of their
whitish color. Finding white mealworms among others,
therefore, is normal and a sign that your mealworms
are growing up.

Lindsay, 3rd grade
Baxter Community School
Baxter, Iowa

11

Why do some mealworms turn black?
Does that mean they're dead?
If you are keeping mealworms you will occasionally find
blackened worms, and if you examine them you will
notice that they have died, dried, and shriveled. With
death comes a change in color. Healthy mealworms are
yellowish to tan in color, except during molting (see the
previous question) and, of course, healthy mealworms
are active and move about.

Chad, 3rd grade
Baxter Community School
Baxter, Iowa

12

What's the difference between black ants and red ants?
Ants come in many colors. Usually, if you see ants of
different colors, you are seeing different species (kinds)
of ants. But there are also many different species of black
ants, many species of red ants, and ants of other colors

and combinations of colors. One very common ant around the home is simply called the little black ant because of its color and tiny size. Another black ant that is very large and is common in the forest is known as the black carpenter ant because it excavates nests in wood. There are also red carpenter ants. Many people think that all red ants are fire ants, but fire ants are not always reddish, and there are many kinds of red ants just as there are many kinds of black ants.

6th grader
Wyoming Center for Teaching and Learning
Laramie, Wyoming

13 Are there any insects that are bioluminescent?

Yes, there certainly are. The most famous are fireflies, which are not flies at all but beetles that have special chemicals that are mixed inside their light-producing organs and produce a cool light, or bioluminescence. They use their lights and special flashing patterns for courtship and attracting mates. Some use their light flashes to fool other species, and after they lure them close they eat the other unsuspecting firefly.

Katie, 5th grade
Manor Heights Elementary School
Casper, Wyoming

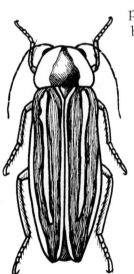

The firefly is actually a beetle that is bioluminescent.

14 Why do ladybugs have spots?

Spots on ladybugs are marks of different species or kinds. There is more than one kind of ladybug, and each has its own special set of characteristics. Some ladybugs are solid colors, and some have spots. They have different numbers of spots and different patterns of spots.

28

Do Bees Sneeze?

The multicolored Asian lady beetle may have from zero to nineteen spots.

Spots and other markings on insects may help insects recognize each other and tell one another apart from other kinds of insects. They certainly help the entomologist to tell one kind from another. Spots may also be part of the insect's warning system (see question 5).

Kayla, 4th grade
Anthony T. Lane Elementary School
Alexandria, Virginia

15 How can you tell how old a ladybug is?

A ladybug is an adult when it looks like a beetle, which means it will not grow anymore and that it is at least a few months old. Ladybird beetles grow from eggs that hatch into larvae in the spring and summer; by fall they are ready to move to hibernation spots. They will hibernate as adults and

> You cannot tell age by the number of spots. The spots don't change with age. Once a ladybug becomes an adult it may live for just a few weeks or in some cases live over the winter. A one-year-old is a very old ladybug!

then start laying eggs again the following spring. So, if you see a ladybird beetle in the early spring it may already be a year old. If you see one in the summer it is probably just a few weeks or a few months old.

Dustin, 2nd grade
Linford Elementary School
Laramie, Wyoming

16 How can you tell how old an insect is?

It is not always easy to know the age of an insect, and there is no simple rule to follow because of the many kinds of insects that exist. Some insects, like many flies, have a very rapid life and go from being an egg to an adult in a matter of weeks. Others, like several aquatic,

29

Appearance

or water-inhabiting, insects, may take several years to grow from an egg to an adult. Or, as with some cicadas, an insect may take up to 17 years to become an adult.

The easier thing to learn is to recognize and tell an adult insect from a young insect. If you see an insect with fully formed wings that is able to fly then the insect must be an adult. There is no such thing as a baby or immature insect that can fly. Many people make the mistake of calling small flies babies and larger flies adults, when in fact they are just two different kinds of flies. A young fly is a wingless maggot or larva, and the adult fly is winged. Once an insect is winged it is an adult and stops growing. If the insect is a wingless type or one with small wings as an adult, then telling young from adult is trickier. The only perfect way to know the age of an insect is to raise it and observe it.

Sarah, 4th grade
Henderson Elementary School
Cheyenne, Wyoming

17 How can you tell how old a butterfly is?

Many butterflies do not live very long once they have changed from a caterpillar to an adult butterfly, so guessing the age is not too difficult. Many butterflies live just a few weeks during the spring or summer, just long enough to feed on some nectar and reproduce. If you

Other butterflies may live longer, so their age may not be as obvious. Some, like the monarch butterfly, migrate or travel great distances in their lifetimes and spend winters in southern California or Mexico and move northward in the summer. The monarch you see in the summer may be in its second year of life or may be newly hatched. The mourning cloak butterfly lives a long time too and has the unusual habit, for a butterfly, of hibernating beneath objects during the winter. It is one of the first butterflies to appear in the spring. Therefore, if you see a mourning cloak some spring or summer day, it may be nearly a year old.

Do Bees Sneeze?

see a brightly colored butterfly with perfect, undamaged wings, then it may be only a few hours or a couple of days old. Butterflies that have lived for several days or a few weeks may show more wear and tear, with damaged and ragged wings, peck markings from birds that tried to eat them, and with dulled colors or worn scales.

Mark, 3rd grade
Manor Heights Elementary School
Casper, Wyoming

18 Why are some bugs slimy?

A lot of people think of insects as disgusting, slimy creatures, but actually most insects are not slimy at all. They may appear slimy or slick because of their shiny exoskeleton and the smooth waxy layer that covers it. But if you touch them, you will discover that they are dry, not slimy. There are some insects that are a little slimy, especially when young or immature. There is a fly called a black fly whose larvae live attached to rocks in rapidly moving streams. Black fly larvae may be found in dense clumps and feel slimy like the slick moss or algae you may also find on the rocks. Other insects may appear or feel slimy because of the slimy stuff they live in. Insects in gooey mud, rotting debris, and animal guts could certainly seem slimy.

Megan, 2nd grade
Greenvale Park School
Northfield, Minnesota

19 Why do flies' eyes look like boom box speakers?

That's a pretty good comparison! A compound eye is so named because it is actually an aggregation of hundreds or thousands of individual parts called facets. The facets seem to give some texture and design to the insect's eyes and make them look like boom boxes. Some insect eyes are quite colorful with a rainbow of colors in the

31

Appearance

facets reflecting brilliantly in the sunlight. When we look at an insect in the eye we don't see a single pupil looking back at us. Instead we see the hundreds or thousands of facets.

Nick, 3rd grade
T. Roosevelt School
Oyster Bay, New York

20 Why can't you see some insects' eyes?

There are several possible explanations for not being able to see an insect's eyes. Some insects do not have eyes, and some insects have eyes that are quite small. Immature or young insects like caterpillars may have a set of very tiny eyes that are nearly impossible to see without a magnifying glass or microscope. However, many insects have eyes that are large enough to see, but they are hidden by a camouflage of color or body parts. Some insects have hairy eyes! Numerous whiskerlike hairs cover the compound eyes of certain insects, making them a little difficult to see. Some insects have their eyes sunken in pits or hidden beneath ridges and bumps on their heads, so that you have to observe from a funny angle to spot them. Many insects have eyes that are the same color as the head; they blend in perfectly. Especially on dark- or black-headed insects, a dark or black set of compound eyes can be difficult to see. Frequently, you can see the eyes, but it's hard to

The insect's compound eye is made up of many miniature eyes.

Do Bees Sneeze?

make out the outline of the eye, so it's difficult to know where the head ends and the eyes begin.

Ashley, 2nd grade
Charles Quentin Elementary School
Lake Zurich, Illinois

21

How can you tell a male from a female insect?
Telling male and female insects apart is easy to do with some kinds and very difficult with others. The easy kinds are those that have special body parts, colors, or behaviors that belong to just one sex. For example, if you see or hear a cricket chirping, you will know it is a male because the male sings to attract his

> There are many insects, like certain wasps, in which one sex may have wings and the other is wingless. The common velvet ant is really a wasp whose females are wingless and antlike and whose males are winged.

mate. The same is true for the cicada, and on the underside of the male cicada's abdomen you can easily see his large flaplike tymbals, or sound-producing organs. The female cicada can also be recognized by her own special organs. She will have a needlelike ovipositor (oh-vah-pause-ah-tor), or egg-laying device, located under the abdomen and running down the middle, rear part of her body. Other female insects may have easily seen ovipositors too, like the sword-shaped ovipositor of the katydid or the long thread and stinglike ovipositor of the ichneumon (ick-knew-mon) wasp. The male rhinoceros beetle has a large horn that the female lacks, and the male dobsonfly has huge pincerlike jaws, perhaps half the length of his body, whereas the female has small jaws. In many insects, like damselflies, the males have brighter colors than the females. It is also common for the female of many insect species to be larger than the male in order to hold lots of eggs. A female cockroach is easily spotted when she has her egg case sticking out of her abdomen.

33

Appearance

If an insect does not have such obvious features as these, it may take careful observation, study, and knowledge to determine the sex. Proof of sex can be gotten by cutting open an insect's body and looking for its male or female reproductive organs, but even this requires special knowledge of insect body parts and functions.

Kimberly, 5th grade
Starpoint Intermediate
Lockport, New York

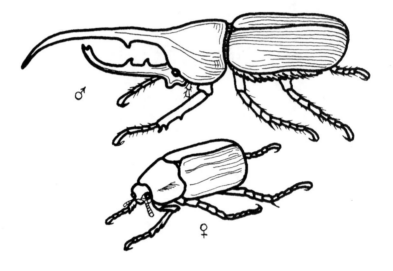

The rhinoceros beetle is an example of a sexually dimorphic insect; the horned males look different from the hornless females.

22 What would a bug look like if it was cut open?

Just as there are many kinds of bugs that look different on the outside, so too are there bugs that look different on the inside. The inside of a caterpillar looks different from the inside of a flea. But even with all of the differences, there are many similarities. If you cut open an insect you would find blood, guts, muscles, and a big open space called the body cavity. You would also see nerves, air tubes for breathing, and maybe some fat if the insect has been eating a lot. You would also find a brain and a heart. You can read more about some of these parts in Chapter 3.

Jacob, 4th grade
Henderson Elementary School
Cheyenne, Wyoming

23 How can you tell if your mealworms will have babies?

It is not easy to tell if an adult female mealworm is pregnant, but it is easy to tell if your mealworms will have babies by watching their behavior. If the adult beetles are mating, then it is almost certain that eggs will be laid and baby mealworms will be on the way. Mating adults are easy to spot, because you will see beetles on top of other beetles in piggyback fashion. Chances are good that babies will be born when mealworms are kept in a proper place with adequate food. They reproduce well.

Catherine, 3rd grade
Baxter Community School
Baxter, Iowa

Rearing Insects

It is fun and interesting to rear insects and watch them grow from egg to adult. Many kinds can be easily fed and maintained in a clean environment and with little space or materials needed. Among the easiest to keep are mealworms and crickets.

A simple container for rearing mealworms containing wheat bran and potato slices

Rearing Mealworms

Mealworms, named for the wormlike larval stage, eat wheat bran and other cereals and grow into the adult darkling beetle. They can be purchased from pet stores, bait shops, or biological supply stores. You can begin rearing large numbers with just a few (6 to 12) mealworms. Place them in a jar or other suitable container and cover them with about 2 inches of wheat bran. Keep the jar sealed but ventilated, at room temperature or slightly warmer for faster growth, and dry to prevent mold. The only moisture needed can be provided by placing a small slice of potato in the container every few weeks or whenever the previous slice has dried or been eaten. The wheat bran will be their primary food and when it is mostly reduced to a fine powder you can discard the dust and add fresh bran. When you separate the powdery dust from remaining bran and live insects, use a small household strainer so that tiny eggs and larvae will not be completely lost.

Mealworms will thrive in these conditions and, if allowed to reproduce, will increase rapidly. You will be able to observe all stages of larvae, pupae, and adult. You will be able to observe how they feed, reproduce, and behave with each other.

Rearing Crickets

Common field crickets can be kept in a container with clean soil, a source of moisture (wet sponge or cotton ball) and a variety of foods. They eat raw potato slices, lettuce, dog food, and other combinations of fruits and vegetable material. Experiment with different food choices, but be careful to test one food at a time and feed in small quantities. Large amounts of food will quickly get moldy, and if you give them large portions instead of small portions you will not be able to tell what has been eaten. As with mealworms, their container should be kept at room temperature or slightly warmer and be sealed and ventilated. In addition to observing the growth and development of crickets, you will enjoy their chirping songs and special ways of selecting mates.

Playing Insect Charades 2.2

The popular party game, charades, can be adapted to the study of insects and be used as a fun class activity.

Organizing Teams and Challenge Lists

Organize the class into 4- to 6-member teams (you can have as many teams as you want) and have each team create a large list of challenging entomology terms, insect names, insect biology concepts, or anything else related to insects and entomology. They should try to identify terms or short phrases that would be difficult for the other teams to act out and guess during the charade. Developing the challenge lists is educational in itself.

Rules of the Game

Each team will have 2 minutes to try to guess another team's challenge item. The goal of the game is to guess the precise insect word or phrase in the briefest amount of time. The team that has the lowest accumulated time at the end of the game wins. Each team member takes a turn to do an insect charade, or act out without any sound a challenge item selected by the opposing team. Gestures in place of words and sounds can be used as clues for the guessing team. All teams can try to guess the answer, but each will take its turn in challenging other teams and in selecting a team member to do the charade.

Examples of Insect Charades

Any insect or insect-related topic or theme is fair, but try to be creative in selecting a challenge list. Imagine the fun and the dif-

Do Bees Sneeze?

ficulty the opposing team may have in acting out the following insect charades:

- lightning bug
- cocoon
- entomology
- Lyme disease
- metamorphosis
- stink bug
- honey bee swarm
- pitfall trap
- doodlebug

Appearance

3 Body Parts & Functions

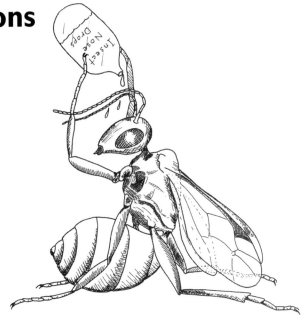

Do insects have teeth?

Some insects that bite and chew solid food, such as plant-feeding caterpillars and grasshoppers, have two strong jaws that may have teeth to help bite and chew. Their jaws are called mandibles (man-dah-bulls) and may have rows of sharp teeth that resemble a saw blade. These teeth are not like ours. They do not grow from gums and have roots. There are no baby teeth that are replaced by adult teeth. They simply have a right and left jaw, each of which may have an edge with a toothlike bump or several toothlike bumps that help the insect cut into and through solid food.

2nd grader
Charles Quentin Elementary School
Lake Zurich, Illinois

2

Do fleas have teeth?

Fleas bite, but they don't have teeth. They have a type of mouth that's called a piercing-sucking mouth. It is like a beak or needle that can stab or pierce skin and then suck blood. It is made of several small pieces that fit together to form a piercing beak and a strawlike sucking device. There are other insects that have similar piercing-sucking mouthparts; some for piercing plants and sucking sap, others for stabbing insects and sucking their blood. The flea is a parasite, or insect that lives on and feeds off the bodies of other animals without killing them, and its mouth is a perfect tool for its way of life.

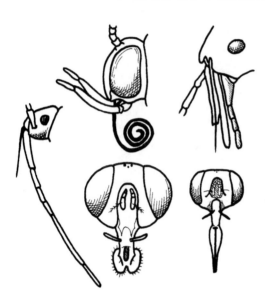

Insect mouths have a variety of forms and functions.
Top row, left to right: piercing-sucking, siphoning, blood sucking
Bottom row, left to right: sponging, cutting-lapping

Tom, 5th grade
Starpoint Intermediate
Lockport, New York

3

Do flies have teeth?

House flies have a mouth that works like a sponge to soak up liquid foods. They do not have jaws or teeth that can bite or a beak that pierces and sucks like a mosquito. Therefore, house flies cannot bite people. If you have something tasty on your skin, however, they might sponge you a little bit. There are other flies that look like house flies and bite people. One of these is the stable fly. They are common around livestock and can bother us with their bites. They may come indoors or be active around the house, so it is easy to confuse them

Do Bees Sneeze?

with house flies. But if you are being bitten by a fly, I promise it is not a house fly.

Daniel, 4th grade
Anthony T. Lane Elementary School
Alexandria, Virginia

4 Do flies really throw up when they land?

House flies have a mouth like a sponge for sopping up liquid foods, and they have feet that can taste, just as we taste with our tongue. When they land to feed, they'll walk in the food to taste it, and if it tastes good they lower their sponging mouth and begin to soak up the liquid food. If some of the food is not watery enough, they will add lots of saliva and thus seem to be throwing up, in order to soften the food for their sponging mouth. They are not airsick and don't really throw up when they land. It's all part of a house fly's unusual table manners.

Ryan, 5th grade
Starpoint Intermediate
Lockport, New York

5 Do bugs spit?

Probably the most notorious insect spitter is the grasshopper, which many people say spits tobacco juice (see question 6).

There is another insect famous for spitting, but it is unrelated to the grasshopper and spits in a most unusual way. The spittlebug is a type of plant hopper whose young produce huge globs of spittle. You may have noticed these

There are many other insects that have salivary glands and therefore produce saliva or spit, but they may use the spit for different purposes. The paper wasp uses its saliva or spit to make its nests. Its saliva is mixed with plant material just as we mix water and glue with newspapers to make papier-mâché.

43

Body Parts & Functions

spittle masses during the summer on plants in fields and meadows. The watery, bubbly spittle comes out of the spittlebug's rear, not its mouth, helps it hide from enemies, and keeps its body moist.

Tim, 2nd grade
Charles Quentin Elementary School
Lake Zurich, Illinois

6 How do grasshoppers make the tobacco juice?

Of course grasshoppers don't really make tobacco juice; they simply spit a substance that looks like tobacco juice as a defense mechanism when they are disturbed. This juice is the watery undigested food that is stored in their crop, which is part of their gut. So the grasshopper is just vomiting part of its gut contents up, which happens to be a reddish brown fluid that resembles tobacco juice.

Dustin, 5th grade
Starpoint Intermediate
Lockport, New York

7 Do bees have a mouth?

Bees certainly do have a mouth, and so do all other insects, but a bee's mouth is quite unusual. The honey bee has what's called a biting-lapping mouth, because it has two biting jaws and a long lapping tongue. Its jaws are strong for biting and chewing solid food, like pollen, and for chewing wax to build its wax hive combs. Its tongue is actually four separate tongues that are held close together for lapping up nectar, honey, and water. The bee has a small upper lip and a small lower lip, but bee's lips do not look at all like people's lips. After food enters the mouth it goes down the bee's throat and into the gut.

Nick, 3rd grade
T. Roosevelt School
Oyster Bay, New York

Do Bees Sneeze?

8

How does a bee make beeswax?

Bees have special wax glands as part of their skins. Small, thin, delicate flakes of wax come from these glands, and the bee chews them in its mouth to soften and shape the wax for making wax honeycombs for storing honey and wax brood combs for raising young bees.

4th grader
Henderson Elementary School
Cheyenne, Wyoming

9

Do insects have throats?

Insects have throats, but they don't have tonsils or that little thing called a uvula (youv-you-lah) that hangs down over the top of our throats. An insect's throat may be called a pharynx (fair-inks) or an esophagus (ah-soff-ah-gus). The pharynx is the tube or passageway directly behind the insect's mouth, and the esophagus is the longer tube behind it that leads to the insect's stomach. Actually, the insect throat can look very different in different insects and work in different ways. In some insects, like cicadas, aphids, and others that suck plant juice, the pharynx is large and muscular and works like a powerful pump. In other insects, the esophagus may be the main part of the throat and works as the main road for food to go from mouth to stomach.

Katie, 2nd grade
Charles Quentin Elementary School
Lake Zurich, Illinois

10

Do insects sneeze?

Insects do not have noses with nasal passages and sinuses as we do and therefore can't get tickles in their noses or clogged airways to make them sneeze. (They don't get boogers either!) They do not breathe through

45

Body Parts & Functions

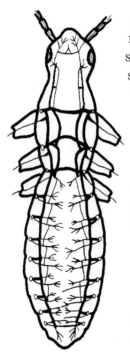

a nose or a mouth, and they do not smell with a nose. For these purposes they have other special structures. The insect's antennae or feelers are somewhat like a nose because many insects use their antennae for smelling (see question 11). The special structures used for breathing are hollow tubes, called trachea (tray-key-ah), which branch out throughout the inside of the insect's body and little holes in the sides of their body, called spiracles (spear-ah-culls), so that air can go in and out of the trachea. If you look carefully along the sides of an insect body you might be able to see little dots on the left and right side of each section of the abdomen. These are the spiracles, and they resemble little windows that can open and close to let fresh air in and used air out. The air enters each spiracle and then travels throughout the trachea, which branch out like the branches of a tree, delivering fresh air to all parts of the insect body. Insects don't need lungs to breathe because the spiracles and trachea do the job for them.

Insects breathe with their tracheal system—branching, hollow tubes that deliver oxygen to all parts of the body.

6th grader
Wyoming Center for Teaching and Learning
Laramie, Wyoming

11

Do bugs have noses?

In question 10 I talked about this, but I will add a bit more. The insect's antennae are like a nose because they can detect odors. Insects use their antennae to smell the world around them. Flower-visiting insects use their antennae to find the scent of pollen and nectar. Insects that feed on garbage and filth certainly find their antennae useful in detecting the smelliest and foulest things. Insect antennae help to smell the scents given off by other insects, and in this way insects can locate their mates, their enemies, and their nestmates, as in the cases of social bees, ants, and wasps. Insects use their antennae to follow scent trails and to avoid poisons and other hazards in nature.

46

Do Bees Sneeze?

Even though they don't have noses like ours, insects' antennae serve them well. In fact, in a smelling contest between insects and people, insects would win, because their antennae are far more sensitive to a much wider

Insect antennae come in all shapes and sizes. Generally those insects with large and fancy-looking antennae are very likely to be excellent "sniffers" and rely on their sense of smell perhaps more than their eyesight and other senses. Those insects with tiny antennae probably depend more on sight and other senses to get along in the world. Just by examining the structures of insects closely, you can often guess what kind of lives they lead.

range of smells than our noses are. There are odors that insects can detect that we cannot. The human nose is no match for a good pair of insect antennae.

Casey, 3rd grade
Manor Heights Elementary School
Casper, Wyoming

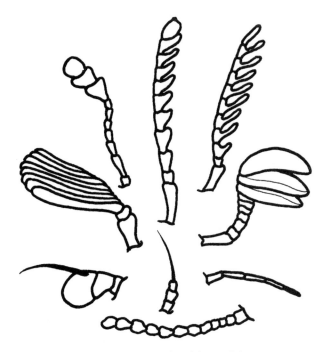

Insect antennae come in a variety of shapes and sizes.

Body Parts & Functions

12

Do insects cough?

Because insects don't have lungs (see question 10) they do not have to cough to clear out mucous and moisture that can collect there. Insects have a throat, called the esophagus, and sometimes insects will clear their throats by spitting up, but this is not coughing—it is regurgitation.

3rd grader
Manor Heights Elementary School
Casper, Wyoming

13

Can insects have hiccups?

Hiccups cannot occur in insects because they don't have a throat designed like ours and because they don't breathe through their mouths. A hiccup is a sound that people make when there is a little spasm in our chest accompanied by the passage of some air.

5th grader
Manor Heights Elementary School
Casper, Wyoming

14

How many eyes do flies have?

Flies have two, large compound eyes on the sides of their heads and three simple eyes called ocelli (oh-cell-eye) on their foreheads. The compound eyes (called that because they are composed of many smaller parts—see question 15 for more details) allow them to see objects, shapes, color, and much of their surroundings, whereas the simple eyes are believed to detect darkness and light. They all work together to help flies survive. The compound eyes of

Do Bees Sneeze?

flies are usually quite large, often occupying most of the head—"all the better to see you with."

Robert, combined 3rd and 4th grades
Hutton Elementary School
Spokane, Washington

15 Do insects have good vision?

Insects that have large or well-developed compound eyes (see question 14), such as bees, flies, and dragonflies, have excellent vi-sion, but insect vi-sion is not identical to human vision. They can see most of the colors that we can see, but they can also see ultraviolet colors that are invis-ible to us. So when a honey bee searches for food she is using flower colors that we

> The other thing that you will notice about many insect eyes is their large size. Those with eyes nearly as large as their heads can see in almost all directions because the eyes wrap around the sides, top, and bottom of the head. Ommatidia (the basic units that are aggregated to make up the compound eye) positioned at the back of the head can be detecting things at the same time ommatidia at the front, bottom, or sides are seeing things. That's one reason it so difficult to sneak up on an insect. They are looking almost everywhere at the same time!

can see and flower colors and markings that we cannot see to locate the richest supply of nectar and pollen. Insects can detect different color designs, but they are not very good at telling apart shapes. They are, how-ever, very good at recognizing movement. Being able to see in this fashion helps them avoid enemies and find mates, food, and shelter. The next time you look at an insect examine its compound eyes. If they are large then the insect undoubtedly has good vision and depends a lot upon its eyesight. If the eyes are small then the in-sect relies more heavily on other senses like taste, touch, and smell to move about in its environment.

Robert, combined 3rd and 4th grades
Hutton Elementary School
Spokane, Washington

49

Body Parts & Functions

16

Do insects see color?

Different insects have different abilities to see various colors. The insects with excellent color vision, like the honey bee, can tell the difference between yellow, blue-green, blue, violet, ultraviolet, and purple. Many insects can see ultraviolet, but people cannot. Entomologists believe that most insects see yellows and blues better than reddish colors. Most bees and wasps and many other insects cannot see the color red.

Laura, 4th grade
Anthony T. Lane Elementary School
Alexandria, Virginia

17

Can an insect be nearsighted or farsighted?

Some people become nearsighted (they see close objects well, but they don't see as well at a distance) or farsighted (they see distant objects well but see close objects poorly) because of changes in their eye lens. We wear glasses (artificial lenses) to correct faulty eye lenses. Insect eyes have lenses too, but they are very different in their design and do not undergo the same changes that occur in our eyes. Insects do not age like people either, so they do not become nearsighted or farsighted as they grow older. Insects may have defects in their vision due to injuries, deformities, and perhaps other causes, but it is difficult to know precisely if these conditions ever result in nearsightedness or farsightedness. One thing is certain—you will never find an insect wearing glasses!

Stephani, 8th grade
Laramie Junior High School
Laramie, Wyoming

Do Bees Sneeze?

18

Does every insect have only two eyes?

No, not every insect has two eyes. Some insects, such as worker termites, have no eyes! There are some cave insects that never see the light of day and live in a world of perpetual darkness; therefore they have no need for eyes. They are totally blind and rely on their senses of smell and touch to move about in their caves. Some insects lack compound eyes but have three ocelli (see question 14) to help them

> If we count just the compound eyes and the simple eyes or ocelli, then the greatest number of eyes would be five. But remember that an insect's compound eye is really a collection of many individual eyes or ommatidia. A dragonfly may have as many as 10,000 ommatidia per compound eye. Therefore, if we add up all of the facets of each compound eye and the three simple eyes, a dragonfly would have more than 20,000 eyes!

detect light versus dark and possibly shadowy movement. It is believed that some insects may actually be able to detect light through their skin! A small beetle, called the whirligig, seems to have four compound eyes. The whirligig swims in rapid, crazy patterns on the surface of ponds, lakes, and streams and has its two compound eyes divided in half, so one pair sits atop the head to see things from above, while the other pair sits below the water surface to scan underwater. It looks like a four-eyed beetle, but really it has two compound eyes like those of most other beetles. And finally, there are insects like caterpillars that do not have compound eyes or ocelli but rather a small group of tiny eyes called stemmata

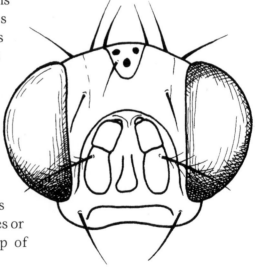

Front view of insect eyes

51

Body Parts & Functions

(stah-mah-tah) on each side of their heads, which probably detect sunlight like ocelli. Do not be confused by those insects that have fake eyes, called eyespots, which are eyelike markings on the body to confuse, frighten, or surprise their natural enemies (see question 24, Chapter 5).

3rd and 4th graders
Hutton Elementary School
Spokane, Washington

19

Do bugs close their eyes?
Insects do not have eyelids like people and are unable to close their eyes, blink, or wink. When an insect is at rest, or when we might think it is sleeping, we are not able to tell by looking at its eyes. Insects are born with eyes wide open.

Deby and Nate, ages 11 and 10
Monument, Colorado

20

Do bugs have ears?
Not all insects have ears, but there are several that have very well-developed ears that are large and can hear well. Insect ears are called tympana (tim-pan-ah). You may be surprised to know that the ears are not necessarily on the head. Some of the best examples of insect ears are those that belong to grasshoppers and crickets. Some grasshoppers have two tympana, one on each side of the insect's body. If you look beneath the wings, on the side of the grasshopper's abdomen, just next to the thorax, you will see a large circular or oval, windowlike structure. It is like our ear drum, a thin piece of skin that covers a hollow cavity. Special nerves connected to this tympanum (the singular of tympana) allow the insect to hear the faintest of sounds and vibrations. Many crickets have a pair of tympana, but they may be located on the front legs! Crickets can hold their legs up

and point them in the direction of the sound that they are trying to hear.

Another good example of an insect with ears is the cicada, or what many people call the locust. The females have huge tympana on their abdomens to hear the courtship songs sung by males, just as crickets and grasshoppers use theirs. The sounds that insects can hear differ from species to species. We can hear some of these sounds, like the songs of crickets, but some moths have tympana so sensitive that they can hear the echolocation of bats, a sound that the human ear cannot detect.

> Some insects have no tympana but are still not hard of hearing. Some of these insects listen with their antennae. The antennae of such insects, like male mosquitoes, are covered with tiny hairs with special nerves that enable them to hear the buzzing and humming of their mates in flight. These are not ears as we think of them, but they serve the same purpose.

Desiree, 5th grade
Starpoint Intermediate
Lockport, New York

21 Do all insects make sounds?

Most insects do not make sounds, as do crickets and cicadas. The deliberate chirps and buzzes for attracting mates are special behaviors belonging to a relatively few insects. There are many more insects that can produce sounds like the buzzing of wings or clicking of body parts. The click beetle, for instance, snaps or clicks its body to spring away from its enemies. But most insect sounds are probably the noises they make during normal activities. And if we had better hearing or if we built an instrument that could listen to the softest of sounds, then we would discover all insects make sounds. They certainly make sounds as they move or perhaps as they eat. Imagine if we could hear the pumping sounds a flea makes as it sucks blood from a body, or the sound of a caterpillar munching on a leaf. The sounds of the

53

Body Parts & Functions

insect world are mostly hidden from us because our ears are not good enough to hear them; but some of the sounds made by insects eating and moving can be heard. There is a beetle called the deathwatch beetle that bores in wood, and on quiet evenings people have heard them banging their heads inside the walls: tap, tap, tap. Sometimes you will hear the sounds of wood-boring beetles inside pieces of firewood as they tap against their tunnel walls.

Marlaina, 4th grade
Henderson Elementary School
Cheyenne, Wyoming

22

Do insects have blood?

Insects have blood, called hemolymph (heem-oh-limph). Insect blood also contains blood cells, as our blood does, but there are many differences between insect blood and human blood. Most insect blood is not red. An exception to this rule is the bloodworm, a tiny fly larva that lives in stagnant ponds and

> A very important and different function of insect blood is to help the insect shed its skin and grow larger. It uses its blood pressure to puff up its body and break out of its old skin and to help the wings expand and other body parts enlarge as the insect produces a new skin.

stinky mud. A chemical called hemoglobin in its blood gives the insect a bright orange or red color. The color of most insect blood is clear, yellowish, or greenish. The blood of insects and humans function differently too. Insect blood does not carry oxygen to the body as our blood does. It is most important for carrying nutrients from food to the body and for helping eliminate wastes. Insect blood plays a big role in keeping the right balance of salts and other chemicals that are necessary for the body's proper function. The blood is a place where insects can store extra food. If an insect is wounded it will bleed, but blood cells will help make a

54

Do Bees Sneeze?

clot to plug up the wound. Insect blood cells will also attack germs and fight some infections as our blood can.

Finally, insect blood doesn't travel through veins and arteries as our blood does. Instead it sloshes around inside the insect body and bathes the inside body parts (see question 24).

Nina, 2nd grade
Charles Quentin Elementary School
Lake Zurich, Illinois

23 How much blood does a beetle have in it?

That depends on the size of the beetle. Beetles can be very tiny or very large, but even the largest of all beetles, the goliath beetle, wouldn't have enough blood to fill a thimble. The blood of most beetles or other insects could be measured in drops or fractions of a drop.

If a grasshopper was to donate blood, you would get only 150,000th of a pint from a full-grown individual. In other words, it would take approximately 150,000 grasshoppers to get a pint of blood.

Lisa, 5th grade
Starpoint Intermediate
Lockport, New York

24 Do insects have hearts?

Insects have several hearts! The insect heart is much different from our own. The main heart of an insect is located near the rear of the body in the top part of the abdomen. It is a tube that looks a little like an uninflated balloon. It has some tiny holes in each side to let blood enter, and it pumps the blood forward through a connecting tube called the aorta. The blood spills out into the insect body cavity near the head and neck and eventually flows back to the heart to get pumped back again. Our heart pumps blood through tubes called veins

Body Parts & Functions

and arteries that extend throughout our bodies. Insects don't have veins and arteries.

In addition to the main heart, there may be some smaller hearts or miniature pumps to push blood into the legs, wings, and antennae. These little extra hearts are found where appendages connect to the body and are important, because without them the insect would have a difficult time getting blood out to the very tips of long legs and long antennae. Therefore, some insects may have 11 hearts: the main heart, six extra hearts for the legs, two extra for the wings, and two extra hearts for the antennae.

Jackie, 2nd grade
Charles Quentin Elementary School
Lake Zurich, Illinois

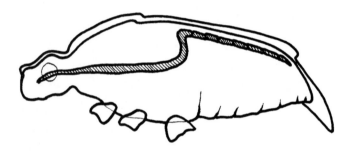

The insect's circulatory system is comprised of a tubelike heart and blood vessel and a large blood cavity in the body.

 How does an insect heart beat?

The insect heart is a muscular tube that can beat 16 to 140 times per minute. It has a lot of little fan-shaped muscles that attach to it and to the body wall of the insect that aid its beating. These muscles stretch and relax, helping the heart refill with blood.

When an insect is moving a lot, or stretching, then the blood gets sloshed around more. Some insects will exercise their abdomens by shortening and lengthening their segments as if they were playing an accordian. This accordian motion gets the blood moving faster and aids the beating heart.

Katie, 2nd grade
Greenvale Park School
Northfield, Minnesota

26 Do bugs sweat?

Insects do not sweat and do not need to sweat, because they are cold-blooded animals, which means their body temperature goes up and down with the outdoor temperature. People and other warm-blooded creatures have body temperatures that don't change with outside temperatures. When it gets hot, warm-blooded creatures sweat, or perspire. The perspiration helps keep the body cool when it's hot outside. When insects are in a hot environment, their body temperatures go up and they become more active. There is no perspiration to cool them. When insects are in a cold environment, their body temperatures go down and they become sluggish, and if it gets too cold they may hibernate.

Caroline, 2nd grade
Charles Quentin Elementary School
Lake Zurich, Illinois

27 Do insects urinate?

Insects that live on land usually need to save or conserve water in their bodies to prevent themselves from drying out. They cannot afford to lose much water when they eliminate wastes from their bodies and thus do not urinate. They eliminate a waste called uric acid that doesn't contain much water. Insects that live in water do not have a water conservation problem. They are surrounded by water and can afford to pass a lot of water through their systems to prevent their bodies from

57

Body Parts & Functions

getting too soggy. They eliminate waste as ammonia flushed out with water.

Insects produce their wastes with organs called Malpighian (mal-pig-he-in) tubules (named after a man called Malpighi). In humans, urine is produced by organs called kidneys. The Malpighian tubules are the insect version of kidneys. Uric acid and ammonia are dumped into the insects' hind gut and mixed with other waste products instead of traveling out the body through a separate tube, as urine does.

Justin, 5th grade
Manor Heights Elementary School
Casper, Wyoming

28 Do insects go to the bathroom?

Except for those insects on a strict liquid diet, like blood feeders, and insects feeding on nectar and plant juices, all insects must get rid of solid wastes. Therefore insects do go to the bathroom (see question 27). Solid insect waste is usually very dry and looks like tiny pellets. Caterpillars, which can consume huge amounts of plant material, leave larger, moister pellets. If there are flys in your house, you may find fly "specks," which look like little grease spots on the windows or countertops where they have gone to the bathroom. Insects that eat wood or tunnel in plants often leave a trail of sawdust or chewed plant material with their body wastes. The solid waste product of insects is called frass.

Doug, 5th grade
Starpoint Intermediate
Lockport, New York

29 Do insects pass gas?

Animals that pass gas do so because they have helpful microscopic organisms (e.g., bacteria) in their guts to aid with the digestion of their food. These bacteria are

Do Bees Sneeze?

able to break down the complex food chemicals into simpler chemicals that will nourish the body. Gas can be one product of these digestive processes. Cows, for example, are great natural gas factories. They consume so much hay and other plant material that they rely on lots of microorganisms to help digest their food. They produce a gas called methane in very large amounts; to get rid of it they burp or pass it out the other end! Insects also have some microorganisms in their guts that assist with digestion; therefore gas may be a natural by-product. Termites are excellent examples of insects that digest a lot of plant material with the aid of microorganisms and they are the number one methane producers among all insects and perhaps among all animals.

Nikki, 5th grade
Manor Heights Elementary School
Casper, Wyoming

30

Do bugs have hair?
Yes, insects have hair of various sizes. Their hairs are called setae (see-tee), and one hair is called a seta (see-tah). Insects may have a lot of setae over much of their bodies, or they may be mostly hairless with just a few setae in scattered spots. There are also different kinds of setae. Some hairs are simple, soft, bristly or whisker-like, and others are stiff and coarse. Insect pollinators, like bees, are typically very fuzzy because their bodies are covered with numerous, branched setae that help in gathering pollen. Some hairs help the insect sense its surroundings. Hairs can be very sensitive to touch and vibration and allow the insect to feel things nearby or objects it touches. Some hairs actually help the insect hear (see question 20). Hairs can be important for insects that live in cold places. Just like a fur coat, the thick hairy coat of a bumble bee keeps its body warm enough to visit flowers on cold and windy days. And some hairs are weapons and used

for self-defense. Certain types of caterpillars have stinging hairs, setae that are hollow like miniature straws, and when the hair is touched a stinging chemical comes out of it that causes the attacker's skin to burn and itch. The saddle-back and puss caterpillars are among the most famous stinging-hair insects.

The color and designs of hairs may also help in defending insects. Butterflies and moths have special flattened hairs called scales that densely cover their wings and bodies like the overlapping shingles on a roof. The dense layer of scales on the wings of butterflies and moths gives them their beautiful colors and interesting patterns. Some of these patterns help disguise them or confuse their enemies.

Katie, 4th grade
Anthony T. Lane Elementary School
Alexandria, Virginia

31 Do bugs have skin or scales?

Yes, insects have skin and scales, but both are different from what we normally think of when we think of skin and scales. The insect's skin is also its skeleton (see question 32). Insect scales are unlike the scales on lizards or fish. Insect scales are special, flattened hairs (see question 30) that cover the wings of butterflies and moths. Some other insects, like silverfish, have a shiny, silvery look because their bodies

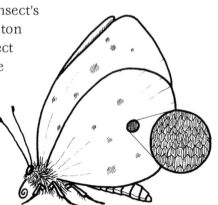

Butterfly wings are covered with flattened hairs, called scales, which add texture and color to the insect's skin.

are covered with scales. Scales help protect the insect's wings and body and may aid in escaping from sticky spider webs. Some people are highly allergic to insect

Do Bees Sneeze?

scales, and if they are around moths and breathe the scales that may be like dust in the air, they will have a sneezing or allergy attack.

Nick, 3rd grade
T. Roosevelt School
Oyster Bay, New York

32

Do bugs have bones?

Bugs don't have bones, but they do have a skeleton. Our bones and skeleton are inside our bodies, covered by muscles and skin, but the insect skeleton is on the outside of the body and covers the muscles and inner body parts. It is also the insect's skin. Because it is a skeleton on the outside of the body it is called an exoskeleton (exo- means "outer"). The insect exoskeleton is like a suit of armor and protects the insect from scrapes, bruises, and bumps. Like human skin, it protects the insect from germs and other harmful organisms that might try to penetrate its body. Muscles attach and are anchored to the exoskeleton to give the insect strength. Also, the exoskeleton is very important for helping land-dwelling insects to conserve or save water. It may have a very waxy layer that keeps water in and prevents the insect from getting wet in a storm. The exoskeleton is divided into sections or smaller segments so the insect can bend its body, move, and have the flexibility to do the things it must do to live. All of the insect's body is covered by the exoskeleton, from the tip of its head to the tip of the abdomen and all the way around its legs, wings, antennae, and even its

An insect's exoskeleton cannot grow as the body grows larger, as our skin does. As an insect feeds and grows, it will grow too large for its own skin and have to shed it. Shedding of the skin is called molting. Insects molt so they can throw away their old skin and make a new, larger skin that they can grow into. It's just like outgrowing your clothes, throwing them away, and buying some new clothes that are a little too big to allow some growing room.

mouthparts. Part of the gut is lined with exoskeleton. Some parts of it may be thin and soft, and some parts may be very thick and tough. The exoskeleton is one of the reasons insects are so successful—because of it they don't need any bones.

Kit, 4th grade
Pleasanton Elementary School
Pleasanton, Texas

33 Do insects have brains?

As surprising as it may seem, yes, insects have brains. In fact, you might even say an insect has three brains, because their brain is divided into three main parts. The brain is found inside the head, with the largest portion at the top. A smaller part of the brain is located in the lower part of the head, just below and behind the insect's throat or esophagus. The upper and lower parts of the brain are connected by a third part that splits in two and wraps around the insect's throat. It really is all one brain, but it's shape and location in the head are unusual. The brain is like the command center for a very elaborate nervous system. It helps the insect see, feel, smell, taste, and sense its environment. It is also very important for all the activities that an insect must carry out. The brain helps the insect with its movements, communication, appetite, growth, and development, and it helps manage almost all of its body functions.

2nd grader
Connor Consolidated School
Caribou, Maine

34 Do insects feel pain?

Because insects have a brain and a fairly elaborate nervous system they are able to react to lots of things. For instance, most insects are very sensitive to touch and pressure, so if something squeezes them or touches them

62

Do Bees Sneeze?

they will quickly move away to avoid the contact. They can also tell when something is too hot and will attempt to escape from being burned. If an insect loses a leg or gets part of its body smashed, it will probably wiggle or act excited. Naturally, when we see insects react this way we wonder if they are hurting and if they feel pain as we do. They definitely react to these things, but because their brain is simpler than ours they are not likely to have the feelings that we do. Their actions are probably more like reflexes, which means the body naturally shies away from danger and irritating things, not because the insect thinks about it but because to do so helps the insect survive. But even if we think insects don't feel pain like we do, that is no reason not to respect them and be kind to them. Usually people who understand insects and other of nature's creatures appreciate living things and do not want to be cruel or hurtful.

2nd grader
Connor Consolidated School
Caribou, Maine

35 Do insects have footprints?

Most insects are too small or too light on their feet to have footprints, but there are some that leave footprints in certain places. One place where insect tracks might be found is on the desert sand. There are ground-dwelling beetles that leave trails in the sand, and there are large desert spider wasps that nest underground. You can see their tracks leading into the nest entrance. Crickets may come out at night on sand dunes and scurry all about the surface. By daybreak, the only sign of their existence is their footprints in the sand, which last until the wind blows them away. Another place to find insect footprints is along the muddy or sandy edges of ponds and streams. Many insects that live near the water's edge will leave their marks as they walk or run about. It is

Sometimes scientists say that insects leave their "fingerprints" behind, but they are not talking about the fingerprints found on people. They are referring to the marks of insects like bark beetles, which tunnel beneath the bark of trees and leave distinctive patterns or pathways where they have burrowed. Every kind of bark beetle creates its own special pattern, or feeding gallery, so an experienced person can look at bark beetle damage and tell exactly what kind of bark beetle fed there. In a way, the bark beetle's gallery pattern is like a fingerprint. In the same way, there are tiny fly maggots and caterpillars that tunnel between the top and bottom layers of leaves. These leaf-mining insects tunnel about and leave a special mining pattern behind. Leaf mines are like insect fingerprints on leaves.

certainly not as easy to recognize which footprint goes with which insect, as it may be with large animals, but it could be fun to try and find the insects that leave their marks in the mud or sand.

3rd and 4th graders
Hutton Elementary School
Spokane, Washington

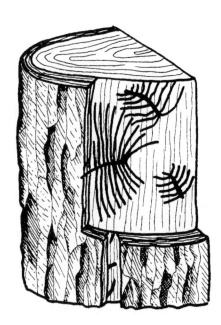

Bark beetles tunnel beneath bark, leaving distinctive, telltale galleries that are much like footprints.

Do Bees Sneeze?

36

If you pull off all of its legs will an insect die?

If an insect had all of its legs removed, it would be unable to move, feed, escape its enemies, and seek shelter. It would be quite helpless and would certainly die. It may not bleed to death, however, because insects do not usually lose a lot of blood when a leg or an antenna breaks off. It would die from its helpless condition. Intentionally pulling the legs off an insect is not something you do if you respect and appreciate living things, and I know that you would not do it.

Kyle, 5th grade
Manor Heights Elementary School
Casper, Wyoming

37

Do insects have belly buttons?

No, they do not. We have belly buttons because before birth we get food and nourishment from our mothers through an umbilical cord. After we are born our umbilical cords are cut. The mark that remains is the belly button. Insect mothers do not provide nourishment to their unborn babies in this way. Most insects lay eggs instead of giving birth to live young (see question 44). Like a chicken egg, all the nourishment for the developing insect must come from the insect egg yolk. There are some insects that give birth instead of laying eggs, but these insect mothers simply keep the eggs inside their body until they are ready to hatch. The young insect still gets its nourishment from the egg while inside the mother's body. The larval tsetse (set-see) fly is an exception; it gets nourishment from its mother, but it doesn't have a belly button.

Lisa, 2nd grade
Charles Quentin Elementary School
Lake Zurich, Illinois

38

Why do bees buzz when they fly?

Bees buzz because their wings are beating so rapidly in flight. They beat their wings hundreds of times per second and when an insect as large as a bee moves its wings that fast, body parts vibrate and give off a buzzing sound. If you listen carefully to the buzzing, you can hear the change from low-pitched buzzing to high-pitched buzzing as the bee works harder to beat its wings faster. Other insects with rapid wing beats may have their own buzzing sounds.

Ashley, combined 3rd and 4th grades
Hutton Elementary School
Spokane, Washington

39

Why do queen ants lose their wings?

Queen ants need to have wings only once in their lives, when it is time to mate and start a colony. Female and male ants that are ready to mate and to start new colonies grow wings for their mating flights. Oftentimes after a rain, when the soil is moistened, hundreds of winged ants will emerge and begin to fly. They fly to find mates and they fly to find new homesites to begin new colonies. Finding a mate and finding a new home does not take a long time for the successful ants, so they don't keep their wings very long. Once mating is complete and they have settled into a new place, their wings are shed and they begin the tasks of building a new colony. Termites have similar behaviors.

David, 2nd grade
Charles Quentin Elementary School
Lake Zurich, Illinois

Do Bees Sneeze?

40

Can ladybugs fly when they are born?

When ladybugs hatch from their eggs they are ladybug larvae—small, six-legged, wormlike creatures without wings. They can't fly as larvae, but after they turn into an adult they'll be able to fly. Almost as soon as they turn from a mummylike pupa into a winged adult, they can fly. It may take a little while for their new adult body and wings to dry and harden, but in a very brief time they can take off in flight.

Mara, 2nd grade
Charles Quentin Elementary School
Lake Zurich, Illinois

41

Do insects have muscles?

Yes, they most certainly do. Flying insects have very large flight muscles in their thoraxes to power their wings. Their leg muscles, for locomotion and grasping, can be quite large too. There are tinier muscles found in other parts of the body too, such as the muscles that cause the heart to beat and the muscles that operate the antennae. An insect, just like a person, would not be able to function if it didn't have muscles throughout its body.

Dana, 4th grade
Anthony T. Lane Elementary School
Alexandria, Virginia

42

How do insects turn into pupae?

Many insects, like beetles, moths and butterflies, fleas, flies, ants, bees, and wasps, go through a series of re-markable changes called metamorphosis; they begin as an egg, turn into a wormlike larva and then into a mummylike pupa, and finally emerge as an adult. To

67

Body Parts & Functions

turn into a pupa from a larva, the insect must stop eating and become quiet. Then its entire body changes shape, inside and out, and turns into a pupa before growing into an adult. It may appear to be resting from the outside, but inside its body parts are changing drastically. This metamorphosis is very complicated and is controlled by chemicals called hormones.

Anna, 2nd grade
Linford Elementary School
Laramie, Wyoming

43 Why do some insects go through only three stages?

Insects that have what's called a gradual metamorphosis start as an egg, hatch into a young insect called a nymph, and then turn into an adult. The egg, nymph, and adult are the three life stages of this insect. Common examples of insects with gradual metamorphoses are grasshoppers, crickets, plant hoppers, aphids, and stink bugs. Insects that have a complete metamorphosis go through four life stages: egg, larva, pupa, and adult. Common examples of these are butterflies, bees, flies, beetles, and lacewings. Some insects have only three stages because they don't change much when they go from their young stage to their adult stage. They change gradually, and the changes are not as spectacular. For example, an adult grasshopper doesn't look that much different from a young grasshopper, except for its larger size and its wings; whereas a butterfly doesn't look at all like the caterpillar it used to be. It changed completely. To make such a complete change requires a fourth life stage, the pupa. The pupa is the extra step needed to change from a wormlike larva to a winged adult. If an insect is not going to make such a big change, then three stages are all it needs to become an adult.

Riana, 4th grade
Henderson Elementary School
Cheyenne, Wyoming

Do Bees Sneeze?

44

Is there an insect that lays eggs?

Most insects lay eggs, and we call the act of egg laying "oviposition" (oh-vah-position). The egg is the first stage in the life of an insect, and mother insects will lay eggs or oviposit in a variety of ways and places. Insects may oviposit a few eggs or thousands of eggs. Some eggs are produced and deposited one at a time, whereas others may be deposited in huge numbers.

> Some flies lay maggots instead of eggs, and many aphids have live births during part of the year. There is one very strange insect, called a sheep ked, which is a wingless, fly-parasite of sheep, that keeps the egg in the body, allows it to hatch into a maggot that also stays in the mother's body, and only lays it when it is ready to turn into a pupa. The pupa soon sheds its skin to become another adult.

Some are scattered without any care on the ground (those of a walkingstick) or in the water (those of a mayfly), others may be placed carefully inside a nest or in the protective parts of plants, like the bark beetle eggs laid under tree bark. Some eggs, like those of cockroaches and praying mantids, are packaged in special egg cases and protected from the weather. Some insect mothers, like the earwig, stay with their eggs and guard them against enemies. The giant water bug father carries his mate's eggs glued to his back until they hatch and can fend for themselves. All insects start out as eggs, but not all insects lay eggs. If that sounds confusing, here is an explanation. All insects come from their mother's eggs, but some mothers keep their eggs in their bodies until the eggs hatch. The young insect hatches from the egg inside the mother's body and the mother therefore gives birth to a live baby, rather than laying an egg.

Dreshard, combined 3rd and 4th grades
Hutton Elementary School
Spokane, Washington

69

Body Parts & Functions

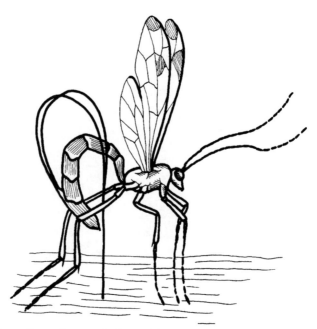

The parasitic wasp is an example of an egg-laying insect. The act of egg laying is called oviposition.

45 Why do insects lay so many eggs?

Not all insects lay a lot of eggs, but those that do are increasing the chances for the survival of their young. There are many dangers facing insects from the time they are eggs to the time they are adults. Weather, accidents, natural enemies like insect-eating birds and mammals, diseases, and food shortages can take a heavy toll. Therefore, if an insect lays a lot of eggs, there is a better chance for at least some of the young to survive and reproduce. Insects that are not careful about laying their eggs or caring for their young usually produce very large numbers of eggs to make up for the expected loss of lives. The insect that provides a very special home for the eggs and young, or cares for its young, may not need to lay as many eggs to be successful.

Marlaina, 4th grade
Henderson Elementary School
Cheyenne, Wyoming

Do Bees Sneeze?

46 What is the chemical ants give off when they leave the colony?

The chemical is a perfume called a trail pheromone (fair-oh-moan). It is a scent that lingers and works as a trail marker for ants to follow. It will help guide ants back and forth from the colony and to new food sources as they are discovered. As more ants join the trail, more trail pheromone is produced, so the marker gets even stronger. Ants and other social insects make other kinds of pheromones that help them communicate with and take care of one another.

Victoria, 5th grade
Starpoint Intermediate
Lockport, New York

Hatching Insect Eggs

An Insect Egg Hunt

Begin this project by purchasing some insect eggs from a biological supply company, or better yet, by exploring and collecting your own insect eggs from nature. Some eggs, like those of praying mantid and cockroaches, are easily identified by the hardened cases the mother constructs to protect her eggs. Other eggs, like those of squash bugs and stink bugs, can be easily found on plant leaves because they are laid in large clusters. Look on plants, under ground cover, and in other sheltered places where insects live. Pay careful attention to the type of plant on which eggs are found, because insects usually lay their eggs on the plants that they like to eat.

Incubating the Eggs

Keep the eggs in a clean, dry place where they will be undisturbed. If you keep them at or near normal outdoor temperatures, then they will probably develop and hatch at their normal time. Sometimes you can speed up the process by keeping them at room temperature or a little warmer.

Preparing for the Blessed Event!

Be ready when eggs hatch, because the young insects will be hungry. You will need to supply them with an adequate amount of fresh food or be prepared to release them where they can obtain food naturally. If you hatch insects that eat other insects, then the task of feeding becomes even more challenging. You may discover that insect predators will turn into cannibals if they stay close together.

Hatching Insect Pupae
Finding Insect Pupae and Cocoons

You can collect insect pupae or cocoons (cocoons are protective covers that contain pupae) and hatch them in much the same way as hatching eggs. Look for pupae or cocoons buried in the soil, beneath ground cover, in leaf litter, or in other protected places. A butterfly pupa, called a chrysalis, will be suspended by a silken stalk on the underside of plants, structures, fences, and other objects that offer some protection. Cocoons may also be attached to the stems and leaves of trees and shrubs.

Caring for the Insect

When you collect a pupa, chrysalis, or cocoon, it is not only important to keep it in a dry, protected place but also to keep it in the same position as you found it. If it is a chrysalis hanging from a twig, do not remove it from the twig, but keep it hanging freely in a cage or jar. If it was found laying on its side, buried or hidden beneath soil, place it in the same position with its protective coverings. Also, place a stick or similar object in the cage or jar so the insect that emerges will have a place to climb and stretch its wings. Pupae placed in unnatural positions and adults without adequate room to dry their wings may not survive.

As with eggs, a pupa may need a long time to hatch, or if kept at warmer temperatures may emerge early. Early emerging adults may be difficult to care for, because their natural foods may not be present and the season has not advanced.

Walking Like an Insect

(An Ideal Activity for Groups of Three)

Have you ever wondered how a six-legged creature like an insect walks? It is not as simple as walking with only two legs. The insect has to coordinate four extra legs in the most efficient manner possible, and, as it turns out, there is one best way for a six-legged creature to walk. This activity project will help answer the question and involves observing insects and imitating their walking pattern.

Choosing a Walk

Think about the different possibilities for walking with six legs. Would it make sense for the insect to move all the legs on one side and then the other in a left-right-left alternating pattern like ours? Or would it perhaps be better to move the front pair of legs first, followed by the middle pair, followed by the hind pair of legs? As you think about the possibilities (drawing a picture can help) make a guess about what the best pattern would be, and think about the reasons you decided on this pattern.

Practicing the Insect Walk

With two partners, stand in a line and pretend each of you is a part of the insect's thorax, each with a pair of legs. One person will be the front pair of legs, the other the middle pair, and the third person the last pair. Try to walk in the pattern that you have described.

Observing the Real Thing

Having made a guess and modeled your walk, let's test it by observing an insect in action. For observing an insect's walking pattern, a large, relatively slow-moving insect is best. The Madagascar hissing roach is an ideal test subject and may be available

74

Do Bees Sneeze?

from pet stores or biological supply houses. Place the insect on a light-colored sheet of paper on a flat surface and try to determine the order and manner in which it moves its legs. Can you see the pattern? You may have to coax your insect to move or you may have to slow it down.

Solution

If successful, you saw the insect pick up three legs at a time, alternating the movement of one set and then the other set. The insect lifts the front and back legs on one side of its body at the same time as the middle leg on the opposite side. When these three legs come back into contact with the surface, the other three legs lift up. In so doing the insect walks with two tripods, or three-legged structures. When the left tripod is on the ground, the right tripod is in the air, hence the insect is always supported by the most stable structure—a three-legged tripod. They do not rock back and forth and their motion is pretty smooth and energy efficient.

Now, walk as an insect really walks!

Designing an Insect Leg

This project teaches the parts of an insect leg and how legs can be adapted for different kinds of functions and types of locomotion. First, let's examine a basic insect leg.

Five Basic Leg Parts

With an illustration or an actual insect as a guide, try to find the five basic parts of the insect leg. It's easiest to start at the insect's foot. The foot, or tarsus, is usually made up of several small subunits (1–5). Each tarsal segment gives some flexibility to the insect foot and allows for a better foothold. Many insects have a pair of claws at the end of the foot to aid in traction or grasping. Also, each tarsal segment may be equipped with little padlike structures for added grip.

The second leg part is the tibia, or lower leg. It is joined to the tarsus and is usually the longer, well-developed leg segment. It is all one piece. It may have hairs, spines, or other ornaments associated with it.

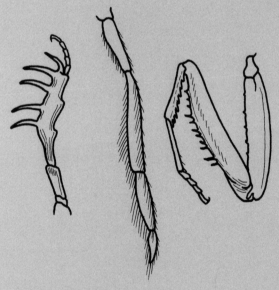

Insect legs have specific forms for specific functions. Left to right: digging leg of scarab beetle; swimming leg of back swimmer; grasping leg of praying mantid

76

Do Bees Sneeze?

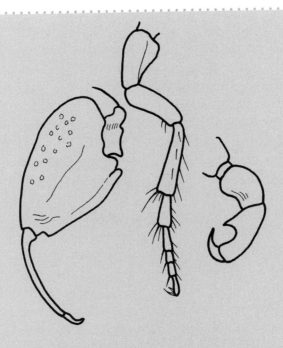

Left to right: grasping leg of water bug; jumping leg of flea; clinging leg of louse

The third leg segment is the upper leg, or femur. It too is one piece and usually large or well formed. You may notice that insect anatomy sometimes uses the same names as human anatomy.

The fourth leg segment is a tiny part that may be difficult to see. It is a short piece between the femur and the base of the leg that attaches to the insect body. It is called the trochanter, and it adds one more flexible piece to the five-piece leg.

The fifth segment, or coxa, is like the ball in a ball-and-socket joint. It is small and fits in the body socket. It allows the leg to rotate or move in different directions from the body. It is the leg's anchor to the body.

Customized Insect Legs

From this basic insect leg design, you can design many special legs for special purposes. Insects have evolved this way: they can use their legs for swimming, jumping, digging, grasping, clinging, or simply walking and running. For a leg design project, you can try a couple of things. Try to imagine what a leg designed for swimming would look like. Would it have short, heavy segments and be rounded, or would it be long, smooth, flat, and streamlined? Draw a basic insect leg and then draw a leg (using the same five leg parts) that will be an excellent swimming tool (hint: many insect swimmers use their legs like oars). After you have designed the perfect swimming leg, find a swimming insect or a picture of one and compare your design with nature's design. What parts of the leg have been modified? How have the leg parts been modified and why does the design make the insect a better swimmer than a walker or a runner?

The same challenge of designing the perfect insect leg can be done for the other types listed above (jumping, digging, etc.) because there are examples in the insect world for all of them.

Another approach to this project is to first examine different legs from some unfamiliar insects, using actual specimens or photos or figures, and try to guess what the leg is best designed to do. Can you guess that an insect is an expert digger by looking at its legs? Can you spot an insect that preys on other insects just by looking at its front legs? Most insect legs that are customized for special functions can be properly matched to that purpose with some close observation and critical thinking.

Remember that there are some unique insect legs. Dragonflies and damselflies have legs that look like a basket for catching insect prey in flight. Their legs are excellent capturing devices, but they are not much good for anything else except for grasping a twig or other object when the insect rests.

By examining insect legs only, it is often possible to guess where an insect lives, what it eats, and how it behaves.

Do Bees Sneeze?

4 Size, Strength, & Speed

What is the smallest bug in the world and how small is it?

Fairyflies, which are not really flies but actually tiny wasps, are among the smallest of all known insects. The adult fairyfly may be less than 1 millimeter (smaller than 1/16th of an inch) in length. They are so small that they can live inside other insect's eggs! They are insect egg parasites that attack other insects by feeding within their eggs.

1st grader
Shadow Hills School
Alpine, California

2

What is the largest bug and how big is it?
Among the largest insects in the world are the goliath beetles of Africa, which are nearly 100 millimeters or 4 inches in length. They have heavy bodies about the size of a person's fist! They are the tanks of the insect world and winners of the heavyweight class.

1st grader
Shadow Hills School
Alpine, California

3

What is the longest insect in the world?
Among the longest insects in the world are the tropical walkingsticks. The spiny walkingstick of Australia is 25 centimeters in length, almost a foot long! The largest insect ever to have lived is a now-extinct species of dragonfly with a wingspan of nearly 2 feet.

Dreshard, combined 3rd and 4th grades
Hutton Elementary School
Spokane, Washington

Walkingsticks are the world record holders for being the longest insects.

4

Why are insects small?
Small insects have the advantage of living and hiding in small, hard to find and hard to reach places, and therefore are well protected from the weather and their

80

Do Bees Sneeze?

enemies. Insects come in a variety of sizes, and being small often means you don't have to compete or struggle against those insects that are much bigger than you. Small creatures also require smaller amounts of food and water to survive.

4th grader
Pleasanton Elementary School
Pleasanton, Texas

5 Why are some insects so big?

Some insects are large because their large size allows them to go places and eat things that small insects cannot. The fact that there are so many different kinds of insects, of different sizes, is one of the very interesting things about insects.

2nd grader
Linford Elementary School
Laramie, Wyoming

6 How big are insect eggs?

Insect eggs come in a variety of shapes, sizes, colors, and designs. You might think that big insects have big eggs, and that little insects have little eggs, but this is not always so. Some of the largest insect eggs are those produced by skinny walkingsticks. The walkingstick egg can easily be seen with the naked eye, and under a magnifying glass or microscope it may appear to be quite fancy. Many have little bumps, ridges, and other markings on the outside and look like little Christmas tree ornaments; some look like miniature urns or pitchers; and many resemble seeds. They may be only a millimeter or two in length—some produced by large tropical walkingsticks are $6^1/_2$ millimeters long (about $^3/_8$ inches)—but they are large compared to most insect eggs. The walkingstick female lays her eggs one at a time. Other insects, like cockroaches and praying mantids,

81

Size, Strength, & Speed

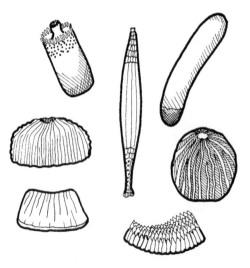

lay their eggs in cases. The cases can be large, but the eggs hidden inside are small. The smallest insect eggs belong to tiny insects like parasitic wasps, flies, gnats, midges, springtails, aphids, and mealybugs. There are some insects that lay their eggs inside the eggs of other insects! These tiniest of eggs are only a fraction of a millimeter in length and have just a little bit of yolk.

Examples of insect eggs and egg cases

Jessica, 2nd grade
Charles Quentin Elementary School
Lake Zurich, Illinois

What is the fastest flying insect?

The fastest flying insects are probably flies. Although there are many speedy flies, the record probably belongs to a group of flies called bots and to the horseflies. These flies are believed to fly as fast as 25–30 miles per hour. That may not seem very fast to us, but for a small insect in flight, that's really zipping along. For comparison, a honey bee flies at about 14 miles per hour, and the fastest dragonfly may cruise at 18 miles per hour.

Another speed record held by flies is the number of wing beats per second. Most flies beat their wings hundreds of times in a single second. Some small midges beat their wings more than 1,000 times a second! They too are fast-flying insects, but wing speed alone does not determine how fast they can go.

Robert, combined 3rd and 4th grades
Hutton Elementary School
Spokane, Washington

Do Bees Sneeze?

8 What is the slowest insect alive?

There are several insects that live quiet, slow-moving lives, but the group that is famous for its lazy lifestyle are the scale insects. Scale insects are small insects that live most of their lives anchored or attached to a plant leaf, stem, root, or fruit and sit motionless as they suck plant juices. They have very tiny legs when they're young and they crawl about looking for a place to settle down, but once they leave their crawler stage they hunker down to feed and move very little. Some even lose the use of their legs. These would be among the slowest insects alive.

Scale insects spend much of their time anchored to plants, appearing more like a blemish than an insect.

There are also insects like lice, bots, and warbles, which are parasites on and inside the bodies of animals and birds. A bot or warble is like a big maggot. It has no legs and likes to burrow under the skin where it lives off its host animal. They do not move once they settle down. When it does move, it moves with its body, since it lacks legs, and slowly wiggles and pulls itself along.

Dreshard, combined 3rd and 4th grades
Hutton Elementary School
Spokane, Washington

9 How fast can a water spider move?

The insect known as the water strider or water treader is sometimes called a water spider. They have a

83

spiderylike appearance and skate rapidly and wildly on the water's surface (see question 2, Chapter 5). I am not sure anyone has measured their speed in miles per hour, but it's obvious from watching them that they can move very quickly over short distances. If you have ever tried to catch one in your hands or even a net, you know how quick and elusive they can be. They may not be the fastest insects, but they are certainly one of the best speedsters on the water surface.

Lisa, 5th grade
Starpoint Intermediate
Lockport, New York

10 How strong are ants?

Ants are capable of lifting and moving other insects or objects much larger than themselves. An ant may be able to lift and carry things that weigh 20 times its own weight. You may remember seeing an ant or several ants dragging a big grasshopper back to their nest. This seems quite amazing when we think of how much we weigh and how much we can lift. If a 50-pound girl or boy were as strong as an ant, then (s)he could lift 1,000 pounds, or a half-ton. That means you could pick up a horse! Ants also work together as a team to move even larger objects.

Brit, 3rd grade
Baxter Community School
Baxter, Iowa

11 How come bugs have so much energy?

Many insects seem full of energy. So many buzz around us, while others fly at great speed. Social insects like termites, ants, and bees work long and hard. Insects always seem to be on the go. They get their energy from

Do Bees Sneeze?

nutritious foods. Insects with long and busy lives will have to eat a lot or store a great deal of food in order to keep up their busy pace. If they run low on food or water, they will run low on energy.

Another thing that causes insects to be more energetic is the weather. When the environment gets warmer, so do insects (see question 26, Chapter 3), and as they warm up, their movements become quicker and they appear more lively. Colder weather slows them down and energy is conserved. Therefore, on warmer days when insects are naturally more active, they will have to use more food to remain active. Adequate food, water, and warm temperatures give insects much energy.

3rd and 4th graders
Hutton Elementary School
Spokane, Washington

12 Do insects use a lot of energy to fly?

It takes quite a bit of energy to fly, and insects definitely use a lot. They have to be healthy and well fed in order to fly well, to fly strongly, and to fly great distances. They have huge flight muscles in the thorax, which take a lot of energy to work. Some insects can save energy for their flight muscles by using their skin, or exoskeleton, to help fly. The wings attach to the exoskeleton and the exoskeleton bends and clicks to help the muscles move the wings up and down.

3rd and 4th graders
Hutton Elementary School
Spokane, Washington

13 Why do stag beetles have such big jaws?

Male stag beetles have jaws much larger than female stag beetles and appear dangerous and capable of giving a good bite, but actually they are not vicious biters. A bite by a female would actually pinch harder than the male's bite. These beetles are called stag beetles because

85

Size, Strength, & Speed

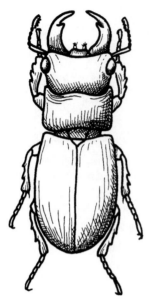

Stag beetles are characterized by large foreward-projecting jaws.

the large teeth of the males remind us of the large antlers on a male or "stag" deer. Like animals with antlers, the stag beetle uses its antlerlike jaws for combat or shoving matches with other males. It seems to be part of their courtship behavior and a way to win a mate.

4th grader
Anthony T. Lane Elementary School
Alexandria, Virginia

14 How high can insects fly?

Most insects fly close to the ground or close to the tops of the shrubs and trees in their area. Some migrating butterflies fly great distances and more than 100 feet in the air. Sometimes small- and weak-flying insects get swept upward and are carried by the winds. If this were to happen you would see insects thousands of feet in the air, but this is not how high insects fly on their own.

Ryan, 5th grade
Indian Paintbrush Elementary School
Laramie, Wyoming

15 How many miles can ants walk?

It depends on the type of ant. Some ants stay closer to their nest than others, and some roam great distances every day in search of food. The army ants, which do not have permanent homes but keep moving their colonies from place to place, can cover miles of territory over a season. They may only travel 100 meters (about the length of a football field) in a daily outing, but that distance is multiplied many times in the life of an army ant.

Fritz, 3rd grade
T. Roosevelt School
Oyster Bay, New York

Do Bees Sneeze?

ppreciate and have some fun with insect locomotion you may
t to have some insect races. Just about any flightless insect
work, as long as you can handle it safely and with ease. Meal-
m adults and many other beetles, ants, crickets, certain cock-
hes, and caterpillars are good.

he best racecourse is a flat surface on which you draw a large
e (24 to 36 inches in diameter) for a finish line. Start the race
lacing two competitor insects in the center of the circle. Keep
n in place with an overturned jar, and when ready, lift the jar
see which one makes it first to the outside finish line. Some
cts are speedy, some slow. Some will go in a straight line, and
e will wander all over before crossing the finish line. If your
ct needs coaxing, try gently blowing on it. Be ready to catch
r insect at the finish line or else you may find yourself in a
 to pick it up before it escapes!
n your mark ... get set ... GO!

5 Behavior

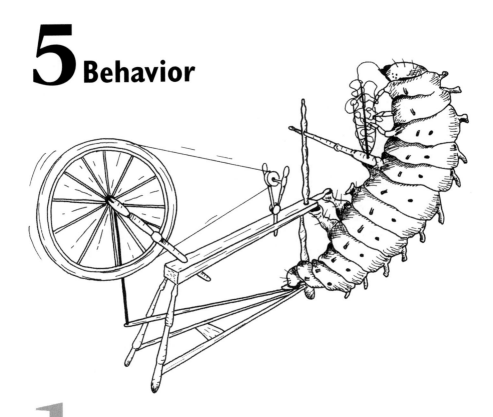

Can insects swim?
Many insects are aquatic insects, which means they spend much of their lives in watery homes such as lakes, ponds, streams, creeks, rivers, and so on. As you might guess, some of the best insect swimmers are aquatic insects, and the ways that they swim are varied and fascinating. Many of these insects swim well because their legs are specially designed to look and work like oars. The water boatman, for example, moves speedily and gracefully through the water with its oarlike legs. Their cousins, the backswimmers, have similar legs and a body shaped like a boat. They swim upside down on their backs, propelled by the strong oarlike motion of their legs. There are many other insects like giant water bugs and diving beetles that are excellent swimmers too. Young dragonflies, called naiads (neye-adds), are jet-propelled. They have three little spines at the tip of their abdomen, surrounding the anus, that work like valves

to let water in and let water out. In an emergency the dragonfly naiad sucks water into the anus and blows it out with enough force to jet through the water. Their cousins, the damselflies, have three paddlelike structures that look like swim fins on their tails, and they swim by wiggling their bodies and fanning these fins. The fins are actually gills (like those of fish) so they are used for breathing as well as for locomotion.

Nonaquatic insects, like those living on the ground, on plants, or in the air, don't have special devices for swimming and therefore can't swim or are not very good swimmers. Some, like grasshoppers and plant hoppers, after accidentally falling into the water, can kick and struggle on the surface and may find their way back to safe, dry land. Others, like many of the flying insects, are trapped by the water surface when they fall in and are quite helpless.

There are also many aquatic insects that don't have swimming legs or special jets or swim fins but still manage to move about without difficulty. Several swim by simply running or scurrying through the water, like an insect dog paddle. Some choose not to swim but to creep and crawl on submerged objects underwater. Some burrow in the mud or sand, build or find shelters in which to hide, and avoid swimming or moving about altogether.

Ellie, 5th grade
Starpoint Intermediate
Lockport, New York

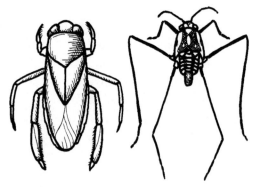

The water boatman (left) is a good swimmer while the water strider (right) is a good surface skater.

Do Bees Sneeze?

2 How do water bugs walk on water?

These water bugs are called water striders and water treaders (some people call them water spiders, but they are insects, not spiders). They are the insect champions when it comes to walking or skating on water. They are also practically impossible to sink or even make wet. The reason has to do with some special unwettable hairs that cover their legs and body parts and with the waxy covering on their outer skins or exoskeletons. Their long, skinny, stiltlike legs keep them off the water surface, and specially designed feet with unwettable hairs keep them dry and prevent them from sinking. There is a very unusual water strider that actually lives out on the open ocean. It is the only insect to live on the sea and it skates equally well on the ocean surface.

4th grader
Henderson Elementary School
Cheyenne, Wyoming

3 Do most insects like water?

Many insects actually live in the water (see question 1), and those that live on land often seek shelter or homes where there is some moisture. Insects have to be very careful about getting too dry. Their small bodies must have water to live, and without shelter from the hot sun, water in their diet, or moisture in the places they live, they would dry up and die. Some insects like more water than others. The insects of the deserts are experts at getting by with the tiniest amounts of water. They get much of the water they need from the foods they eat, and they are very careful about avoiding the hottest parts of the day. They conserve the limited water that they have. Some insects like to drink water. Butterflies siphon water from the edges of ponds and streams, and bees and wasps gather water to drink and to cool their nests.

Laura, 2nd grade
Charles Quentin Elementary School
Lake Zurich, Illinois

4 Why do stink bugs stink?

Many insects stink to defend themselves from natural enemies. There are several insects that people may call stink bugs. One of these skunks of the insect world is the true stink bug, a member of the order of insects called Hemiptera (hem-ip-tir-ah) or true bugs. This stink bug has special glands on its body that give off the bad odor. They stink bad enough for you to notice the scent on your hands after handling one, and it will take a good washing with soap and water to eliminate the stink. The stink is probably stronger and yuckier to smaller animals like the birds or mice that might otherwise want to eat the bug. A relative of the stink bug is the squash bug, which feeds in groups on squashes, cucumbers, and zucchini. In large numbers, their odor is quite noticeable and unpleasant.

> The bombardier beetle, smaller and reddish and blue in color, not only releases a stinky substance from its rear but actually makes a popping sound and a miniature cloud of smoke as it does. Its smell is not as strong, but they are impressive when you catch a bunch in a jar and they all start popping, smoking, and stinking together!

There are also several beetles that stink for self-defense. One such beetle, often misnamed a stink bug, is the circus beetle. This beetle and many of its closest relatives are medium-size, shiny, smooth, black beetles that walk slowly and clumsily along the ground. When disturbed, they raise their rear ends in the air like a skunk, threatening to spray. If bothered further, they pass a stinky chemical from their rear that is strong enough to scare off enemies. Sometimes the enemy outsmarts the circus beetle. A small desert mouse likes to eat these beetles and does so by quickly grasping them with their front paws and then jamming them rear first into the desert sand so the beetle can't spray. The mouse then eats the beetle from the head end and avoids the stink.

Dustin, 2nd grade
Linford Elementary School
Laramie, Wyoming

5 Do ants have a scent?

Actually all ants have a scent, and each kind of ant has its own special scent so that other members of their colony can be recognized and told apart from unwelcome guests or invading insects. People cannot smell most of the ant odors, but some ants give off a stronger perfume than others. Many ants have a chemical in their bodies called formic acid that may give the ant a strong odor or bitter taste. Other kinds of chemicals give off different odors and tastes, some strong, some weak, some sour, some sweet. I guess you could say that ants come in a variety of flavors!

Patrick, combined 3rd and 4th grades
Hutton Elementary School
Spokane, Washington

6 How do insects fly?

Flying insects have two or four wings attached to the thorax that can move at remarkable speeds over amazing distances (see question 7, Chapter 4). Strong flight muscles allow the wings to move, and the

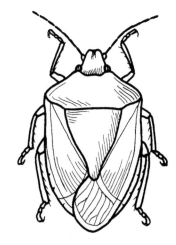

The true stink bug.

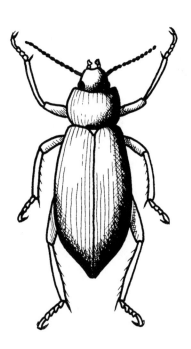

The circus beetle, sometimes referred to as a stink bug.

thorax, which can be somewhat elastic like a rubber band, can help click the wings up and down.

Warren, 2nd grade
Linford Elementary School
Laramie, Wyoming

7

How many types of bugs can fly?

The majority of insects belongs to groups with wings. Just because an insect has wings doesn't mean it can fly, but most that have them, use them. Of the one million named insects, over three-fourths or 750,000, are winged and flying types.

6th grader
Wyoming Center for Teaching and Learning
Laramie, Wyoming

8

Do cockroaches fly?

There are cockroaches without wings, cockroaches with shortened or stubby wings, and cockroaches that have full-size wings. Those with stubby wings or no wings cannot fly. Those with full-size wings may be able to fly, but usually choose not to, preferring rather to walk and to run. However, there are some winged cockroaches that will fly, but their flights are usually brief and over short distances. They are not distance fliers like many other insects. Sometimes those that choose not to fly can be forced to fly by lifting their feet off the ground. If held in midair with its feet not touching anything, the cockroach will beat its wings rapidly, as if it thinks it should be flying because its body and feet are off the ground.

Supreet, 2nd grade
Charles Quentin Elementary School
Lake Zurich, Illinois

Do Bees Sneeze?

9
Can a flea fly?

No. Fleas are insects that never have wings, even though we believe their ancestors were related to flies. They are totally wing-less insects and rely on their jumping legs and a streamlined, flattened body for moving within dense forests of hair or feathers. They live as parasites on their animal and bird hosts (perhaps your pet cat, rabbit, or dog) and actively crawl and jump about. They are quick and powerful jumpers too. They can easily hurl them-selves from pet to pet and onto you and back again. A fa-mous insect scientist named Wigglesworth has said that if a man had the jumping power of a flea he could jump 800 feet high! (Wigglesworth 1964, 57)

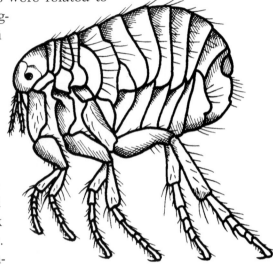

The flea is a powerful jumper.

Patrick, combined 3rd and 4th grades
Hutton Elementary School
Spokane, Washington

10
Why do moths fly around lights?

Moths and many other insects are attracted to light, but this may not be the complete answer to why moths fly around lights or sometimes fly in a spiral to their death in a flame or fire. Some have guessed that night-flying insects tell direction by the position of the moon or the stars or in some way use distant light as a navigational tool or landmark. Nearby lights seem to confuse or mess up their ability to fly in straight paths, and as they continuously try to correct their flying direction,

95

Behavior

they end up spinning out of control toward nearby lights.

Tom, 5th grade
Starpoint Intermediate
Lockport, New York

11

Why do bugs buzz in your ear?
Insects do not intentionally buzz in our ears, although at times it seems that they are doing it just to be annoying. The sound of a mosquito in your ear is not very pleasant when you are trying to sleep. We often hear insects buzzing in our ears because they are attracted to our heads or faces. A lot of biting gnats, midges, and flies are attracted by our breathing and like to bite us on the neck and face, or around the ears. When they are flying close to our heads, their high-pitched buzzing can be heard, and it may sound like they're actually buzzing in the ear.

There are times when an insect accidentally flies into our ear and buzzes like crazy trying to get unstuck, but these are just insect accidents that might happen while you are riding a bike or playing outside and don't realize that you are in the middle of an insect flyway.

Kaitlyn, combined 3rd and 4th grades
Hutton Elementary School
Spokane, Washington

12

Do bugs mate?
Some do and some don't. Those that do mate sometimes do so in the most bizarre ways, and those that don't can be just as mysterious. Male and female insects of many species may mate without much fanfare. When they are mature, and near each other, matings occur. Nevertheless, they are careful and mate only with insects of the

96

Do Bees Sneeze?

same species. Other insects may have fancy behaviors and appearances to attract their mates. Many of the bright colors insects display help them recognize their own species. Some have fancy markings that are flaunted to attract a mate. There are peacock flies that have beautifully pictured wings that they wave about while doing special dances to attract a mate. Some other flies, called dance flies, not only do a special dance, but the male fly captures and kills a tinier insect to offer his prospective mate as a food gift. Another does the same but wraps it in a little ball of silk so the female has to spend more time with him to unwrap her gift. Still another type of dance fly plays a nasty trick on his mate. He offers her a large hollow ball of silk which she unwraps while he mates with her, but by the time mating is complete she discovers her present is empty!

Mysterious as it may seem, some insects don't mate because there are only females and no males. Certain tiny wasps and other insects less familiar to us are able to produce eggs that hatch into a new generation of insects without males. Only females exist and they reproduce fine on their own. Males have become obsolete in these species!

In addition to food, dances, and displays of color, most insects use perfumes or attractive odors to lure a mate. Some moths can smell their favorite perfume at distances greater than a mile.

Several groups of insects improve their chances for mating by forming swarms. Large groups of male midges, mosquitoes, mayflies, caddisflies, and other insects dance like insect clouds on the wing. Nearby females are attracted to these flying swarms and fly toward them to be captured by a watchful male.

Insects unusual for their mating positions are the dragonfly and damselfly. The male grabs the female by her neck with the tip of his abdomen, and she curls her abdomen in what's called a wheel position, joining the tip of her abdomen to the base of his. Here she receives a packet of sperm to fertilize her eggs. They

may fly in the wheel position for several hours and mate in flight. Another interesting mating act is found with the praying mantid. The female may bite off the male's head and eat him in the act of mating.

Cherie, combined 3rd and 4th grades
Hutton Elementary School
Spokane, Washington

Damselflies mating in the wheel position.

13 Does the praying mantid have many babies?

The praying mantid female lays her eggs in egg cases, and the number of eggs is different for different kinds of praying mantids. Some may have more than 200 eggs in a case (Borror, Triplehorn, and Johnson 1989, 227). If they were all to hatch successfully, then the praying mantid would have more than 200 babies.

3rd grader
Manor Heights Elementary School
Casper, Wyoming

14 Are bugs smart or dumb?

If you mean, "are insects intelligent like people and do they have high IQs?" then the answer would be no. If you mean, "are insects clever, witty, and bright?" then I guess the answer is also no. They do not have the brain power to make conscious decisions and they are not aware of things in the way that people are aware. But they do have the powers to find food, places to live, and mates and to avoid certain hazards. They are very resourceful, and their natural instincts have made them extremely successful. They can compete with many other animals and people, and they can dominate others with their numbers and adaptations. Therefore, bugs do not have to be smart to be successful.

6th-grade class
Thayer Elementary School
Laramie, Wyoming

15 Can bees sense danger?

Yes, and they can sense different types of hazards in different ways. One important way bees sense danger is by the smell and by the stinging of other bees. A honey bee will sting in self-defense and in defense of her colony, and when she stings she signals the other bees of her colony with a strong chemical perfume called an alarm pheromone. This perfume is so strong that other bees in the area will become alarmed and quickly come to help. Once one bee stings and sends out her alarm pheromone other bees will be more likely to sense the danger and sting any invader. That's why the more a bees' nest or colony is disturbed, the angrier they get. One sting can lead to another and another until the whole colony is in a frenzy. (Such a place is not a happy place to be.)

When beekeepers enter a beehive and start moving bees around they are very careful not to pinch or disturb the bees too much or else they will accidentally alert bees to danger and make them angry. One way beekeepers calm their

Bees can also sense danger when a beekeeper or others around the hive move quickly or act nervous. Bees in a colony may become alarmed if they see fast and quick movements around their colony or feel vibrations from their hive being bumped and jostled. That's why good beekeepers move slowly while handling their bees. A person who is scared or nervous may alert bees, not only by nervous moves but also by their breath and body chemicals.

Behavior

bees down is by smoking the beehive before they open it. Smoke is another way bees seem to sense danger, but in this case it works to the advantage of the beekeeper. The beekeeper uses a special device called a smoker that allows her to pump smoke, without fire, into the hive. As soon as bees smell smoke they seem to turn their attention away from the beekeeper and onto their colony. They start feeding on their stored honey and are less likely to attack. Scientists are not certain why bees behave this way, but one idea is that they sense danger when they smell smoke and they begin saving the honey from their hive in case of fire.

Jason, combined 3rd and 4th grades
Hutton Elementary School
Spokane, Washington

16

Do bugs have emotions?

If bugs had emotions then there would be sad bugs, happy bugs, mad bugs, loving bugs, excited bugs, frightened bugs, and bugs with all sorts of feelings. Bugs have feelings, but they are not emotional feelings. Their brains help them sense much of their environment and surroundings, but they are not like human brains that allow room for emotion. Insects are unemotional creatures. We can get pretty emotional about them, but they don't get emotional about us. They go about their daily lives and business without such emotions affecting their behavior. So if an insect bites you it's not because it hates you. Likewise, if a butterfly lands on your head it's not because it loves you. But you can still love it!

Cody, 5th grade
Manor Heights Elementary School
Casper, Wyoming

Do Bees Sneeze?

17

Do insects play?

Insects do not play games or sports, and they don't take recesses to play with friends. Sometimes it might look like insects are playing because of the ways they communicate and come into contact with others, but their behaviors all have very important purposes. Insects behave so as to live, grow, and reproduce. We can play with insects, but they won't play with us.

Brandon, 2nd grade
Charles Quentin Elementary School
Lake Zurich, Illinois

18

Do insects sleep?

Insects, like people and all other animals, need to rest or else they will run out of energy and die of exhaustion. Some insects rest in the day or at night, and some rest for brief periods throughout the day or night (like a nap). Insects at rest may not be exactly the same as people asleep, but their rest does serve the same important purpose of conserving energy and preparing for their next activities.

Anna, kindergarten
Rodger Forge Elementary School
Baltimore, Maryland

19

Do insects dream?

In order to dream you have to have a brain and your brain has to remain active even while you are asleep. Even while your body is at rest, your brain may be very busy handling information that was gathered while you were awake. Insects have a brain and insects take time out to rest. Their brains certainly remain active even when their bodies are at rest, so it may not be too far fetched to suggest that insects dream. When active and alert, an insect brain handles information and works much

Behavior

differently than a person's brain, so the way their brains work at rest must be different too. If insects dream, then their dreams would be more similar to their waking activities, as our dreams are to us.

Deby and Nate, ages 11 and 10
Monument, Colorado

20 Do insects snore?

Insects do not snore because they do not breathe through their mouths nor do they have noses like ours. Therefore, they can't make the snoring sounds that some people and animals make while sleeping. There are other sounds insects can make with air entering and exiting their bodies (see question 27), but snoring is not one of them.

William, 2nd grade
Charles Quentin Elementary School
Lake Zurich, Illinois

21 Does every species of insect communicate?

Entomologists do not know about the lives and behaviors of all the insect species that have been discovered, so it is impossible to answer with certainty. We do know that many species of insects and different types of insects communicate. The best known are the social insects. Ants communicate with chemicals to recognize nest mates, find food, take care of the queen and the colony, and signal danger. Bees are excellent communicators too and even have a dance language for telling others where to find food. Several insects communicate with chemicals and body or wing signals for courtship and mating. Insects may also communicate with sounds, like the chirping of crickets and the buzzing of cicadas, to attract mates or mark their territories. Fireflies and others communicate with flashing lights.

Tarin, 5th grade
Starpoint Intermediate
Lockport, New York

Do Bees Sneeze?

22

How can crickets make noise with their wings?
Crickets have two special devices or tools on their wings that they rub together to produce their songs. One tool is called a file, and the other tool is called a scraper. The scraper, attached to the edge of one wing, scrapes against the rough surface of the file, attached to the other wing. The rubbing of scraper against file makes the chirping sound. The male cricket has these tools because he uses his chirping music to attract the female. The female recognizes the chirps of her own kind of cricket.

6th grader
Wyoming Center for Teaching and Learning
Laramie, Wyoming

23

Why do grasshoppers make that annoying sound?
The annoying sound that you are asking about is probably the sound that some grasshoppers make when they take off in flight. A grasshopper called the underwing grasshopper (because of its bright underwing colors) will snap, click, or rattle loudly as it flies. Sometimes it sounds like a rattlesnake's rattle. The loud sound and flashing color from the underwings is designed to startle enemies and give the grasshopper a head start in its escape. On a warm summer day while walking across an open field you can often hear and see the noisy grasshoppers all around you.

David, 5th grade
Starpoint Intermediate
Lockport, New York

24

Do all insects have protection from enemies?
All insects have protection from their enemies, but the protection of some may not be as good or as special as the protection of others. The simplest protection that

many insects have is the shelter of their homes or habitat. Another common type of protection is escape. Some insects are good fliers; some good swimmers; and some good runners, jumpers, or diggers. Most will simply try to get away from an enemy if they can. Of course, if caught by the enemy, many insects protect themselves with a bite or sting. Having a bad odor or a bad taste is another way insects gain protection.

> Another protective strategy is called mimicry. Insect mimics are insect copycats. They look very much like dangerous insects (insects that sting or taste bad) but are not dangerous themselves. They fool their enemies with their copycat disguises and avoid attack by bluffing.

Some insects have hard bodies, spines, stinging hairs, or other body parts that make them unpopular with their natural enemies. An excellent type of protection is camouflage. Many insects have the color and markings of the ground, the rocks, or the plants where they live. Unless they move, they are practically invisible to their enemies or are mistaken for a plant or a rock. Some tree hoppers look like rose thorns. Some inchworms look like twigs. Some moths look like tree bark. Some caterpillars even look like bird droppings. There are some beetles that look like caterpillar droppings. There is a beautiful praying mantid that looks like a pink flower. Examples of insects that resemble their surroundings are numerous.

Some insects fool their enemies with confusing body structures or body postures. A caterpillar might hold its body in a crooked manner so

Eyespots, or fake eye patterns, are protective devices for some insects.

Do Bees Sneeze?

birds don't recognize the caterpillar's body profile. Other insects have colors, designs, or structures that look like eyes, mouthparts, or antennae on the rear of their bodies so enemies will chase and attack the wrong end. Some insects use bright colors and large fake eyespots to try to frighten their enemies. These are just a few of the ways insects protect themselves, but there are many more fascinating examples.

6th-grade class
Thayer Elementary School
Laramie, Wyoming

25 Do insects hide from enemies?

Insects hide from their enemies in lots of different ways. Some have excellent camouflage and blend in with their surroundings (see question 24). Many insects seek resting sites where they are not easily seen. For instance, if you are looking for insects on plants, be sure to examine the undersides of leaves and stems, not just the tops, because many insects hide underneath plant parts. Many insects hide under rocks, logs, and other natural ground cover. If you uncover these insects they will scramble to new cover as quickly as they can. Almost every nook and cranny in nature is a possible hiding place for one insect or another. Hiding is often the best protection insects have against their enemies.

Jamin, combined 3rd and 4th grades
Hutton Elementary School
Spokane, Washington

26 Do bugs give warnings?

Many insects that have a protective device, like a bite, sting, bad taste, or bad odor, also have warnings to discourage enemies from attacking. The most common warning is color (see questions 5 and 9, Chapter 2), but insects may warn of danger in other ways. Some praying mantids threaten with outstretched wings. The

Behavior

circus beetle, like a skunk, threatens to spray a smelly chemical by raising its rear end in the air. Adult cicadas will fly and buzz toward your face, which seems threatening but really is not. Dragonflies will threaten by flying at you like a dive bomber, but they too are not really dangerous. Warnings sometimes come with actual defenses, and sometimes they are just insect bluffs.

6th-grade class
Thayer Elementary School
Laramie, Wyoming

27

Why do hissing cockroaches hiss?

Hissing cockroaches, also called Madagascar roaches because they are from the island of Madagascar, hiss to frighten their enemies. They force air out of holes in  their bodies, which makes a loud hissing sound. The holes in their body are called spiracles, and it is through these holes that insects breathe, rather than through a mouth or nose like you and me. Hissing roaches are not harmful, and their hissing is only a bluff to try to scare off things that may bother them.

Kim, 2nd grade
Linford Elementary School
Laramie, Wyoming

The hissing Madagascar cockroach makes a hissing sound when it feels threatened.

28

Do some insects fight?

Yes, and some insects like termites and ants may even have soldiers for combat. If ants from one colony invade another ant colony, then there will be a fight among

106

Do Bees Sneeze?

colony members. Termite colonies are often attacked by ants, and the soldier termites have armored heads and huge jaws for fighting. In the honey bee colony there are occasional fights between queens. If two or more new queens are born into a colony, they will fight to the death until only one queen remains to rule the colony. There may also be fights among worker bees and the male drone bees. Drones get thrown out of the nest when winter approaches—you can see them being dragged away by workers.

Fighting of sorts can be seen among insects that do not live in colonies. Some insects, like dragonflies, are very territorial, which means they claim a certain area for food and shelter and will attempt to frighten intruders away. They can get into some fights while flying, es-pecially with other drag-onflies that try to invade their territory, but fight-ing seems to be a last re-sort. They will fly at an intruder and have some exciting and often noisy close encounters, and usually one will back off before a damaging fight begins.

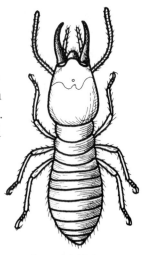

A soldier termite's job is to protect the nest.

Other insects, like rhinoceros beetle males, may have courtship fights and get into shoving matches to win a mate. Fighting is dangerous, and most insects don't fight unless they are trying to capture and eat another creature or trying to keep from being captured or eaten themselves.

Maria, 5th grade
Starpoint Intermediate
Lockport, New York

Do ant armies have wars?

Ants do not declare and fight wars like people, but there are some kinds of ants that have some similar behav-iors (see question 28). One such ant is the army ant. Their colonies have temporary camps, like army biv-ouacs, and remain on the march much of their lives in search of food. They raid insect nests, attack individual

107

Behavior

> Some kinds of ants intentionally raid the nests of other ants and steal their young for slaves. They take the captured young back to their nests and when the stolen ants grow to adulthood, they are put into slavery and work for their master ants for the rest of their lives.

insects, and may even kill and eat larger animals like lizards and young birds that may be trapped or helpless. If one column of army ants meets up with another, then there could be a battle if each army is trying to get the same food.

Mike, 2nd grade
Charles Quentin Elementary School
Lake Zurich, Illinois

30

Are insects attracted to bright colors?

Many insects, especially those that rely on the sweet nectar and nutritious pollen of flowers, are attracted to bright floral colors and designs, which serve to attract a host of insects including many kinds of bees, wasps, butterflies, flies, beetles, and others. The colors help the flower-visiting insects to find their favorite kind of food and the area where the supply is greatest. Insects are particularly fond of the color yellow, but they are attracted to other colors as well. Not all insects are attracted to bright colors, however. Some, like horse flies and deer flies, seem to like large, black or dark objects. Insects of the night are the least interested in colors because they live in a world of gray and black.

Nicholas, 5th grade
Starpoint Intermediate
Lockport, New York

31

How do bees make honey?

Only the honey bee can make honey. There is no such thing as artificial or man-made honey because bees are the only source for this delicious food. They make honey

108

Do Bees Sneeze?

by gathering nectar from flowers with their lapping tongues. They swallow the nectar, which is stored in the bee's "honey stomach" until the stomach gets full or the bee returns to the hive. Once the bee returns to the colony, she spits up the nectar from her honey stomach into the empty cells of the honeycomb (the waxy part of the hive that bees make for storing honey). Before spitting up the nectar, however, the bee added some special chemicals to the nectar inside the honey stomach. The nectar and special mix of chemicals that gets spit into the honeycomb will ripen into honey. When the cells of the honeycomb are filled with ripened honey, the bees put lids on them and save the honey for winter.

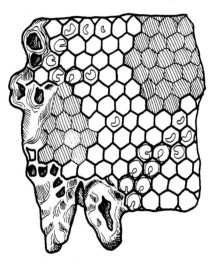

The wax honeycomb in a honey bee's hive contains honey (honeycomb) and young bees (broodcomb).

Tyler, 4th grade
Henderson Elementary School
Cheyenne, Wyoming

32

Why do bees pollinate?
Bees visit flowers because they are attracted to them for food. The foods that flowers may provide are sweet, sugary nectar (see question 31) and protein-rich, nutritious pollen. While bees visit flowers they collect pollen both accidentally and on purpose. A lot of pollen may brush off the flower and stick to the bees' hairy bodies or other body parts. When they visit other flowers, some of the pollen may get brushed off. That's what pollination is—the transfer of pollen from one flower to another. Bees pollinate because they are so good at finding flowers, gathering and hanging onto pollen, and flying to and from so many flowers. Their bodies have special hairs and tools for gathering pollen, and the flowers that they

109

Behavior

visit have special colors, odors, and structures to make it easy for bees to spread the pollen around. If it wasn't for the pollination behavior of bees, many plants could not survive.

Brad, 5th grade
Starpoint Intermediate
Lockport, New York

33 How many times do bees reproduce?

The honey bee queen mates once in her life, although she may mate with several males at this time, soon after emerging from her cell in the colony. She can lay thousands of eggs for several years after. She will lay enough eggs to fully populate a new hive, until a new queen is born to replace her. Worker bees do not normally reproduce.

7th grader
Wyoming Center for Teaching and Learning
Laramie, Wyoming

34 Do bugs have jobs?

Every insect has a role in nature. Each has to do the things necessary for survival and reproduction, which includes finding or making suitable homes and habitats, finding enough proper food, and protecting itself or family members from harm. Some insects, like the social insects (ants, bees, wasps, termites), have specific jobs or duties that help to ensure survival. For example, the queen bee's job is to lay eggs and keep the colony growing. A drone bee's job is to mate with the queen. A worker bee will have several jobs assigned to it, depending upon its age. Younger worker bees are housekeepers and caretakers of baby bees; older workers gather pollen and nectar. Ants and termites have similar kinds of jobs, and some individuals are soldiers and have the job of defending the colony. Some young termites are put to work before reaching adulthood, just like kids who are given chores around the house.

6th-grade class
Thayer Elementary School
Laramie, Wyoming

35 Do insects like the heat?

Some insects prefer cool climates, some prefer warm or hot climates, and some prefer those in between. It depends on the type of insect. One thing is certain: there are insects suited for almost all climates and temperatures on Earth. There are many desert-dwelling insects that prefer a hot, dry climate. There are even more kinds of insects that prefer the hot, muggy heat of tropical rain forests. Many insects become more active when it gets warmer. That's why you can see and collect more insects on a warm summer day than you can on a cool day or a day in winter. When it is warm, their bodies warm up, they move faster, they feed more, and they are busier in their daily chores.

Laura, 2nd grade
Charles Quentin Elementary School
Lake Zurich, Illinois

36 Do all insects emerge in the spring?

No, not all insects emerge in the spring, although that is a very popular time for many insects living in North America. Insects that live near the equator may emerge throughout the year because there is no harsh winter or severe climate to avoid. However, even in northern regions like North America, there are insects that emerge in different seasons. Some insects actually emerge in the winter! There are some small insects called snow

111

Behavior

scorpionflies that can be found on open snowfields during the dead of winter. There are also some very tiny insects called snow fleas (not a true flea but a small, six-legged relative called a springtail) that sometimes have population explosions in the snow during the winter; their millions of pink bodies give a pinkish color to the snow. Winter stoneflies are aquatic insects named for their winter emergences. There are many other aquatic insects that hatch or emerge in the summer and fall. You may notice swarms of mayflies and caddisflies that look like miniature insect clouds dancing and hovering over the water.

4th grader
Anthony T. Lane Elementary School
Alexandria, Virginia

37

How do insects spin cocoons?

Some insects, like moths, butterflies, fleas, and certain wasps, can spin cocoons because they have special silk glands and silk-spinning structures. They make strong silk in their bodies and then spin thin strings of it to surround their bodies when they become pupae. Some cocoons are made of silk combined with leaves and small sticks.

Matt, 2nd grade
Linford Elementary School
Laramie, Wyoming

38

Are bugs messy?

Actually, insects are usually quite neat and keep their bodies and their homes very clean. Even the flies and cockroaches that like to live in and feed on filthy things work very hard to keep their bodies clean. Insects spend a lot of time preening and grooming themselves. You can watch a cockroach carefully clean its antennae by pulling them through its mouth, and they will continue

Do Bees Sneeze?

to rub off dirt and debris from their antennae, legs, and other body parts until they are as clean as possible. Many people say that the roaches in their homes are filthy creatures, but I like to tell them that the cockroaches that live in our homes are only as dirty or messy as the place they live. It is true that some insects can make quite a mess when building nests or feeding. But what may seem messy to us is perfectly natural for the insect. Insects may appear messy at times, but they are not wasteful. They eat the food they gather, and they use only the space they need to live. And insects don't litter! Many insects help clean up the messes we make, and if it wasn't for their help we could be buried in filth and garbage.

6th-grade class
Thayer Elementary School
Laramie, Wyoming

Opening a Window on a Cocoon

Have you ever wondered what changes are occurring inside an insect cocoon as it rests quietly over the winter? Inside, all is not quiet. There are amazing changes taking place in the insect's growth and transformation into an adult. You can observe these fascinating changes by making a window in the cocoon.

Selecting a Cocoon

The best cocoon to use is that of a giant silk moth caterpillar, such as a cecropia moth, Polyphemus moth, or luna moth, but any good-sized cocoon made of silk will work.

Creating a Window

Using a sharp scalpel or single-edged razor blade, very carefully cut a small square window on one side of the silken cocoon. You need to cut all the way through the tough silk cover, but be careful not to go too deep and cut the pupa, which is the insect life stage protected inside. Make a window about 1/2 to 3/4 inches square. Once you have cut it away, place some transparent tape over the opening to protect the pupa from the dry air and dirt. On top of the transparent tape place a piece of dark paper or cloth to block the light.

How and What to Observe

Keep your cocoon in a dry, cool, and protected place, and with any luck you will be able to observe the miracle of metamorphosis as the pupa transforms and emerges as an adult the next spring or summer. Remove the dark cover every week and peek inside to see the pupa. How has it changed? Is the color the same? Does it move? Can you see any adult body parts beginning to form, such as wings or legs?

Teaching an Insect Left & Right

Some insects can be taught to turn left or right after a few simple trials.

Selecting Your Insect

A cockroach or cricket is a good experimental insect, but it is fun to test other kinds of insects as well. You may want to experiment with several to compare results.

Building a Testing Ground

First, construct a simple T-maze. With cardboard, heavy paper, or wood make a walled or enclosed path in the shape of a T. To teach the insect to turn left, place some insect bait (a small, wet, cotton ball or sponge or a small portion of your insect's favorite food [moist dog food is often attractive]) at the top left or right end of the T.

Teaching and Testing Your Insect

Place an insect that has been kept without food or water for at least 24 hours at the base of the T. Allow it to move until it finds the bait. Retrieve it and repeat the experiment until you are convinced that the insect will make the correct turn.

How many times will it take the insect to learn to go up the T and turn in the proper direction to find food or water? Which insects are the speediest learners? Do insects really learn to distinguish left and right, or are they finding the food or water by some other method, such as following a scent?

Letting Insects Choose 5.3

Insects usually have their own specific likes and dislikes, especially when it comes to eating and finding places to live. You can experiment with living insects and learn about some of their food and habitat preferences by conducting choice tests.

Warm versus Cool

Some insects prefer cool places; others like it warm. To determine your insect's preference, take a suitable container that contains the items your insect needs (food, moisture, hiding places, soil, or other suitable substrate) and divide the space in half with a temporary wall of cardboard or wood. Allow just enough space for the insect to move from one side to the other. Place a 60-watt lamp over one side to create a warm side and place the other side against a cool object or in a cool space to keep this space lower in temperature. Be careful to keep all other conditions the same in both sides of the container so the insect will be choosing between a cool place and a warm place, and not going to one side because of some other attractive feature. When your choice test arena is set up, introduce the insect and wait an hour for it to get used to its surroundings. After an hour, or at some other scheduled time, peek in on the insect and record which side of the container it is on. After numerous observations, can you tell if there is a pattern? Has your insect made a choice of warm over cool, or cool over warm? How does what you observed compare to what you know about this insect's preferences in nature?

Damp versus Dry

Set up this experiment in the same way as the previous test, but this time make half of the area damp and keep the other half completely dry. Do not go overboard and flood the damp side or make it so wet that the insect can't get around, but provide enough moisture so it's a more humid environment than the opposite side.

Do Bees Sneeze?

Light versus Dark

Here's another version of the same test, but with one-half of the insect's home kept illuminated and the other half kept in the dark. Remember, be careful to keep all other aspects of the container the same. For instance, don't use a hot light to illuminate one side because this will also make the temperature different on the two sides and complicate your experiment.

You can create other kinds of choice tests for one or more insects, or combine some choices. Try to guess the results of your test before conducting them and ask why the insect should behave as it does.

6 Homes & Habitats

Hive Sweet Hive

1 Where do you find most insects?

Insects can be found almost everywhere, but worldwide the most kinds of insects can be found in the tropical rain forests where there are believed to be more than 1 million undiscovered species. Most insects prefer places where there are lots of hiding places and different kinds of plants and where there is water or moisture. The tropical rain forests have it all.

Cody, 2nd grade
Linford Elementary School
Laramie, Wyoming

2 Why are insects everywhere?

Insects are some of the best-equipped animals for life on Earth. Their small size is an important part of their success (see question 4, Chapter 4), but other insect characteristics have led to their success too. Having wings and being able to fly allow many insects to seek food and shelter over great distances and to escape from enemies, bad weather, and other dangers. The miracle of metamorphosis, where insects can change from a wormlike creature to a flying one, lets the insect live and feed in more than one way. As a grub, a beetle may tunnel in wood, but as a beetle it may fly among flowers and feed on pollen. Special body parts and body functions (see Chapter 3) are very important for permitting insects to live in different places. Excellent senses of smell, taste, vision, touch, and the ability to communicate are advantages insects have over many other living things. They are also successful because they can reproduce so rapidly. Sometimes they breed too rapidly and we see such things as locust plagues. Insects adapt to change very well, so as homes and habitats alter with a changing environment, insects rapidly change themselves to keep up. Being able to hibernate as eggs when the seasons change permit many insects to live in places where it would otherwise be too cold. The fact that many insects are social insects, like bees, ants, and termites, has also contributed to their survival all around the globe.

Kaitlyn, combined 3rd and 4th grades
Hutton Elementary School
Spokane, Washington

3 Do insects have permanent homes?
Some do and some do not. The social insects, which live in colonies, often make their nests or homes in permanent sites. An ant, bee, wasp, or termite nest may last in the same spot for many years, until food shortage, disease, or some major disturbance drives them away or kills off the colony. Groups of tent caterpillars build large silken tents as resting sites and shelters from enemies and the weather. These are permanent homes for the caterpillars until they change into moths.

Do Bees Sneeze?

The caddisfly is an aquatic insect with a larva that may build its own permanent house. Caddisfly larvae make protective cases of sticks, sand grains and pebbles, leaves, and other natural debris that they collect from the stream-bed and ponds where they live. Their cases cover the entire body but have an open front end so they can poke their heads and legs out to move and feed. There is a moth larva, called the bagworm, that does the same thing, except it lives on trees and shrubs rather than in the water. Its bag is home for its entire life.

There are also some insects called gall insects that have permanent homes made for them by plants. Tiny gall wasps, gall midges, and other gall-forming insects lay eggs in plant buds, leaves, and other plant parts. The eggs hatch and the young gall insects feed on the plant, but while this is happening the plant grows a gall, which is a special protective structure that surrounds the insect, giving it shelter for its entire feeding stage. Some galls, like those found on oak trees, are called oak apples because they are as big as apples and look like fruit.

The other kinds of insects that usually have permanent homes are parasites. Parasitic insects feed off other animals and birds while living on their bodies or close to their homes and nests. An unlucky person, pet, or other animal may be the permanent home for biting or sucking lice (also known as "cooties").

Christopher, 5th grade
Starpoint Intermediate
Lockport, New York

How big can insect houses get?

One of the most spectacular and largest of insect houses is the termite castle, or termitarium, that is built in Australia and Africa. These large termite mounds, made of mud and animal manure and baked in the sun, may be larger than a bulldozer and taller than an elephant. They are so tough that in Africa, elephants will rub up against them to scratch. These insect skyscrapers are permanent homes for termites, and they last for many years. Inside, they are divided into hundreds of rooms, like a

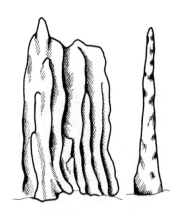

Termitaria, or termite castles, are among the largest insect homes.

large apartment building. The colony lives underground, in the basement part of the termitarium, and in the upper floors as well. The rooms are even air-conditioned! The way the termitarium is built, the arrangement of rooms, and the activities of the termites keep air flowing through the castle and in so doing keep indoor temperatures just right, even when it is scorching hot outside.

Tim, 2nd grade
Charles Quentin Elementary School
Lake Zurich, Illinois

5 Why do some insects live underground?

Why not live underground? It offers the insects that live there a lot of advantages. Insects that live underground are called subterranean insects, and many kinds of insects may be subterranean for part or all of their lives. By living underground insects cannot be seen or easily detected by enemies that may be roaming aboveground. Underground insects can escape harsh temperatures. The deeper they go, the less affected they are by extreme heat and cold. There may actually be food underground for subterranean insects. They may feed on roots, on other underground creatures or eat the rotting leaves and plants that help make up the soil in which they live. A lot of insects dry out easily and, if not careful, can lose too much water from their bodies. It is moist underground, so living there keeps them from getting too dry. There may also be less disturbance belowground. Fire, floods, activities by people, and animals walking all over the ground may not be as much a bother to the subterranean insects as it may be to those aboveground.

Heather, 2nd grade
Greenvale Park School
Northfield, Minnesota

Do Bees Sneeze?

6 Is it true that some insects live for years belowground before being hatched?

Yes, many insects lay their eggs in or on the ground, and it may take several years for the eggs to hatch. Some of these insects are floodplain mosquitoes. When an area is flooded and the water is overflowing the river banks and lakes, floodplain mosquitoes will lay their eggs on land, near the highest watermarks. The eggs remain dormant, which means they are alive but resting, until the next flood. It may be several years before the water gets as high again, so the mosquito lives as an egg on or just below the soil surface, until there is a flood. As soon as a flood occurs, the egg hatches into a larva, or wriggler, grows to an adult, and starts the life cycle over again. If you live in a floodplain mosquito area, this would explain why there are large numbers of mosquitoes after a heavy rainy season.

Many insects lay their eggs underground where they remain over the winter, hatching the next spring. They may be underground for most of the insect's life, but not for years. The insect that is best known for living many years belowground before emerging is the cicada. There are several kinds of cicadas, but the 17-year cicada is the world record

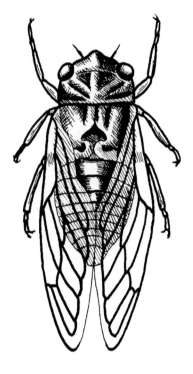

The cicada adult after it has emerged from underground.

holder for life underground. The adult female does not lay her eggs underground but rather in the twigs of trees. Upon hatching, the baby cicada, or nymph, drops to the ground and digs its way underground to begin feeding on the tree roots. Here it remains to feed and grow for 17 years. In its final year it tunnels upward, crawls out of the ground and up the tree trunk at night, where it changes into a winged adult cicada. It lives just long

123

Homes & Habitats

enough to mate and lay eggs to start the next 17-year life cycle.

Jennifer, 5th grade
Starpoint Intermediate
Lockport, New York

7 Do all ants live in dirt?

Many ants live in underground colonies, but ants also live aboveground. Some ants live inside the hollow parts of plants or make special shelters of plant leaves. Some live inside plant galls. Carpenter ants live in wood and logs. Some even have their nests inside our homes. Some, like the army ant, don't have permanent homes and are mostly busy marching from one area to another and make temporary shelters with their own living bodies.

Shauna, 2nd grade
Linford Elementary School
Laramie, Wyoming

8 How far down can ants dig?

Different ground-nesting ants have different kinds of nests. Some may not dig deep, while others build tunnels several feet below the surface. One of the deep-digging ants is the harvester ant, common in the western United States. In deserts and prairies you can see their large nests easily because the ants build a mound with a large clearing around it. The harvester ant constructs a long tunnel, straight down like a mine shaft, with little rooms branching off. The main tunnel may go more than 6 feet deep. Even larger and deeper, however, are the nests of tropical leaf cutter ants. Old colonies are huge with many rooms and tunnels, and the nest may go almost 20 feet below ground!

Fritz, 3rd grade
T. Roosevelt School
Oyster Bay, New York

Do Bees Sneeze?

9

How many rooms do worker ants make?

The number of rooms in an ant nest depends on the
type of ant, just as the size and nature of a nest does.
Some worker ants do not make any rooms, because the
colonies are small and all the ants, from eggs to adults,
live in a small area. Some ants make a few rooms, each
with a special purpose. One room of their colony may
be where food is stored, another room may be for the
queen's chamber, another for her eggs, and still other
rooms may be nurseries where baby ants (or ant larvae)
and pupae are kept and cared for. The largest nests with
the greatest number of rooms are those of the tropical
leaf cutter ant. There are thousands of rooms in the largest leaf cutter ant nests. Some ants have nests divided
into rooms, but the workers don't have to build them. A
tropical tree called the cecropia tree, for example, has
hollow stems with internal walls like room dividers, and
ants make a nest in them. Such plants are called ant
plants because they have hollow stems, hollow thorns,
or other nesting sites attractive to nesting ants. In return
for a nice home, the ants protect the plant from plant-
eating insects and mammals, and from overcrowding
neighboring plants that compete for water and sunshine.

Fritz, 3rd grade
T. Roosevelt School
Oyster Bay, New York

10

What is the purpose of an ant colony?

Being part of a colony is one of the things that ants and
other social insects have in common. Social insects cannot survive alone for very long. They depend on the
cooperation and help of other ants in their colony to
live. So the purpose of a colony is to make sure social
insects have the food, shelter, and protection they
need in order to reproduce. Every member of the
colony has a special job, and only by working together

125

Homes & Habitats

will the colony and each ant survive. An ant separated from its colony will not live very long, and a colony that loses too many of its members may be doomed.

Nicholas, 5th grade
Starpoint Intermediate
Lockport, New York

11

Why do bees live in a hive?

Like ants, bees are social insects and the hive is their colony. They must remain part of the colony to survive (see question 10). Unlike ants, some bees live in human-made beehives, whereas other bees live in nature. Bees in nature may build their hives in the hollows of a tree, stump, or log. Any enclosed shelter, from caves to attics of houses, may be attractive to bees searching for a place to build a new hive. Beekeepers have learned from this behavior how to construct special boxes in which honey bees will nest. The commercial beehive is not much more than an empty box with spaces and foundations for the bees to build their honeycomb and broodcomb (wax cells to contain stored honey and eggs). Bees live in these hives because they offer shelter from the rain, they can be kept at a nice temperature, they are perfect places to raise young bees and feed each other, and they are places where the bees can stay in regular contact with each other. The hive is a place where the colony can grow and prosper.

Stephen, 4th grade
Henderson Elementary School
Cheyenne, Wyoming

12

Do any insects live in water?

Yes, many insects live in water and are called aquatic insects (see question 1, Chapter 5). Approximately half of all the major insect groups (orders) include some aquatic types. Some of the most common and notable

Do Bees Sneeze?

aquatic insects are the mayflies, dragonflies and damselflies, stoneflies, caddisflies, and dobsonflies. There are also many kinds of true bugs, beetles, and flies that are aquatic for part or all of their lives. There is even a moth that has an aquatic caterpillar that lives under silken blankets attached to rocks in rapidly moving water. One of the most unusual aquatic insects is a parasite of freshwater sponges and is called the spongilla fly.

Some insects that live in the water swim freely about. Others live on the water surface and some burrow into the bottom. Many live and hide among aquatic plants and on the surface or under almost any object in the water, from logs to rocks to debris.

Some aquatic insects live in the water for their entire lives, from the time they begin as an egg to the time they become adults. Others may live in the water as young or immature insects and then emerge to become flying adults. Some insects tend to stay close to their aquatic homes where you can see them flying over the water surface or resting on plants near the water's edge. The strong fliers, like dragonflies, may roam for great distances away from their stream or pond but will return to feed and reproduce.

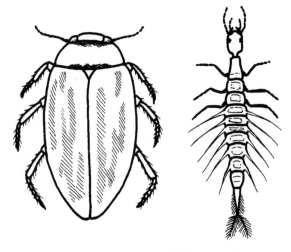

Beetle adults (left) and beetle larvae (right) are among the many aquatic insects.

Jennifer, 5th grade
Starpoint Intermediate
Lockport, New York

13

Where do insects go for the winter?

Some insects, like the monarch butterfly, migrate to warmer climates. Some insects hide in protective places such as under tree bark, under leaf litter, beneath stones, or inside our homes. And many are protected because

127

Homes & Habitats

they overwinter as eggs, or as pupae that may be protected by a cocoon.

2nd grader
Linford Elementary School
Laramie, Wyoming

14 Can insects survive the rain?

When it rains, insects that are flying about visiting flowers, and others that are exposed, will seek shelter to avoid the rain. A small insect is no match for a direct hit by a large raindrop or hailstone. Shelter may be the underside of a leaf or in thick vegetation, under an object on the ground, in a building or other human-made structure, or in any other thing that protects against the wind and the rain. Insects that already live in sheltered places, such as in underground nests, beneath rocks, in logs, and under bark, usually are not disturbed by the rain unless it's a real downpour with some flooding. Even then, some insects are able to adapt. When flooding occurs in fire ant nests, the ants rise to the surface in a huge ball and may actually float with the flood waters until they hit high ground or the water goes down, and then they busily construct a new underground nest. Some insects can get wetter than others and not be harmed. Beetles, for example, with their tough, waxy wing covers and armored body parts, can handle more rain than a delicate butterfly whose wings are useless if they get too wet.

Jason, combined 3rd and 4th grades
Hutton Elementary School
Spokane, Washington

15 What happens to insects in the fog?

Most insects remain at rest during cool, wet weather, so just as they would during rain (see question 14), they take shelter or remain in their homes until it gets warmer and

Do Bees Sneeze?

drier. The insects that live in secure shelters and don't venture outside are not bothered by foggy days at all.

3rd and 4th graders
Hutton Elementary School
Spokane, Washington

16 Do wasps come out of their nests when it rains?

Wasps and other nesting insects will stay home when it rains, especially if it is raining hard or steadily. It would be dangerous to be caught out in the open in a heavy downpour. But just because wasps stay in their nests during bad weather doesn't mean they won't come out if disturbed. In fact, many wasps will hang onto the outside of the nest on a rainy day, if the nest is somewhat protected, and keep a careful watch for intruders. If the wasps are not hanging onto the outside of the nest, they will be alert inside, and a disturbance will bring them out in force, rain or shine. Just because it appears quiet on the outside, doesn't mean no one is home or awake inside.

Miss Eschenburg's 1st-grade class
Almont Elementary School
Almont, Michigan

17 Where do praying mantids live?

Praying mantids live in many places around the world but are especially common or numerous in the warmer climates, like the subtropical and tropical parts of the world. Some very spectacular kinds can be found in tropical rain forests. They are found in the United States too, some of the larger ones in the south and southeastern parts of the country.

2nd grader
Linford Elementary School
Laramie, Wyoming

Homes & Habitats

18

Where do butterflies sleep?

Butterflies rest and seek shelter in thick vegetation where they are protected by leaves and branches, or under objects and inside natural and human-made structures.

Stephen, 2nd grade
Linford Elementary School
Laramie, Wyoming

19

Where do walkingsticks live?

Walkingsticks live on plants where they can blend in and hide among sticks, twigs, and branches. They are among the best-disguised insects because of their sticklike bodies and legs. Walkingsticks live throughout the world, but many of them, and some of the largest, live in the dry areas of the world and in deserts and tropical rain forests.

2nd grader
Linford Elementary School
Laramie, Wyoming

20

Why do bed bugs live in beds?

Many of us are familiar with the expression "don't let the bed bugs bite," which is often said as we get tucked into bed. Actually, there really are insects called bed bugs, and bed bugs may be found in the bed, but they are not necessarily living there. Bed bugs are small, wingless bugs that have an oval-shaped body that is as flat as a pancake. They like to come out at night to feed, and they feed on the blood of people, other mammals, and birds. They have a sharp little beak for a mouth that they stick in like a needle and then suck out their blood meal. Bed bugs that live in homes are probably living in the cracks and crevices of floors, walls, and ceilings or hiding beneath objects where it is tight and cozy. They

130

Do Bees Sneeze?

could be living under the mattress and behind wallpaper. A lot of bed bugs never enter our houses and bother people. Many live in or near the nests of animals and feed on their nest mates. Mud swallow nests that are so common under bridges and elsewhere are favorite homes for bed bugs. The bed bugs like to feed on the baby birds.

Nicholas, 5th grade
Starpoint Elementary
Lockport, New York

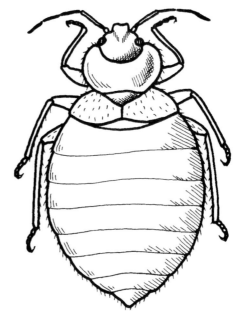

The common bed bug

21 Why do insects come into a house?

Sometimes insects come indoors by accident. They may be crawling, climbing, or flying about and by chance enter through the door, window, or some small crack. Sometimes, we accidentally bring them into the house on our bodies, in suitcases or boxes, on houseplants, with firewood, with pets, and with food. Lights in the house will attract many night-flying insects too. But there are also times when insects come into the house by more than accident. As seasons change, especially in the fall when outdoor temperatures begin to cool, signaling the approach of winter, insects will seek shelter. Our homes are often favorite winter vacation sites for insects that have to get out of the cold. Indoors they can stay warm, and there may even be some food or water in the kitchen and bath, should they need some. Some insects, like the boxelder bugs and earwigs, can make a real nuisance of themselves because they'll often invade our homes in large numbers. They are not attacking us, they just want

131

Homes & Habitats

to be roommates until they can return to the outdoors in the spring. Some blow flies regularly search caves for dead animals—to them, a house is just another cave. Foods in the house can attract certain insects. Cockroaches are masters at sneaking through the tiniest of cracks and crevices and hiding throughout the house, in order to feed on leftover crumbs and unprotected foods. Flies, ants, and other scavenger insects are master home invaders that are attracted by food.

4th grader
Henderson Elementary School
Cheyenne, Wyoming

Do Bees Sneeze?

"Fishing" for Doodlebugs

Doodlebugs, also known as ant lions, are interesting insects that build a cone-shaped pit in sandy soil and lie hidden at the bottom of the pit to ambush unsuspecting prey, such as ants, after they tumble into the pit. The doodlebug has huge pincerlike jaws to grab its prey and suck its blood. If they miss in the first attempt and the prey starts to get away by climbing up the steep slope of the pit, then the doodlebug will start a miniature landslide and make another attempt to grab the trapped insect.

You can catch a doodlebug as you would fish. When you find a doodlebug's conical pit, take a string, small blade of grass, or small stick and gently touch or probe near the bottom of the pit. Get ready! In response to your movement the doodlebug is likely to strike by grabbing the object in its jaws. When it does, pull it up and away from the pit.

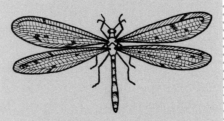

The doodlebug (top) is the larval stage for the ant lion (bottom).

If you are unsuccessful at fishing for doodlebugs, you can try to dig them out. Scoop a handful of soil beneath the pit and scatter it on a screen or in a shallow plate. Be quick, because the doodlebug will rapidly burrow to escape. Look carefully for it to wiggle in the soil you've scattered. They are well disguised and blend in with the soil. It takes a little patience and a keen eye to find them.

Doodlebugs will eat just about any small, unsuspecting insect that tumbles its way. You may want to offer a doodlebug some different food choices to see what it will eat.

Good fishing!

project 6.

Collecting Insect Architecture

Making a collection of insect architecture, like nests and o[ther]
insect-manufactured structures, is an interesting activity tha[t al]
lows some exploration of insect homes, shelters, and behav[ior.]
It is fun and challenging to see how many different types o[f in]
sects and insect architecture you can find. The collection [may]
consist of the actual insect structures or, if that is not possib[le or]
desirable, then a collection of sketches or photos with some [field]
notes. Here are some examples of insect architecture.

Wasp Nests

Wasps make a variety of interesting nests, some of which are q[uite]
remarkable for their architectural designs. Paper wasps, for [ex]
ample, build small to large nests made of paper that they m[anu]
facture by chewing plant materials. Some are simple structu[res]
with a single room or living space for the wasps, while others [are]
large, like multistory apartments with layer upon layer of pa[per]
broodcomb or cells for developing wasps. These nests ma[y be]
found under the eaves and overhangs of buildings and other
man-made structures or may be found attached to trees and o[ther]
natural objects. If you are collecting them, be careful to de[ter]
mine that the nest is abandoned so there will be no danger f[rom]
stinging wasps.

The mud dauber is another wasp that makes interesting n[ests]
of mud. They can be found on buildings, under bridges, and [in a]
variety of natural settings as well. The same caution shoul[d be]
exercised when collecting these nests. Winter is a good time, si[nce]
many wasp nests will not be occupied by adults.

Honeycomb

If you have access to a beehive or can get the cooperation [of a]
beekeeper, it would also be interesting to collect some hon[ey]
comb or broodcomb from a beehive. The design of the cells is [one]
of the most famous examples of precision insect architecture.

134

Do Bees Sneeze?

worms

ther very different insect architect is the bagworm. These moth
rpillars construct bags from bits of leaves off the plants where
 feed and carry them for protection during the entire larval
pupal life. Bags come in various designs depending upon what
t is the source of building materials.

disflies

milar insect architect can be found in the aquatic world.
disflies are insect larvae that construct protective shelters of
es, twigs, sand, or combinations of natural materials for shel-
There are many architectural designs, depending upon the
lisfly species. Some look like miniature log cabins, others like
l shells, and others like cocoons. It's fun to try to find as many
rent types as you can.

t Caterpillars

ther unusual insect architect is the tent-making caterpillar.
se caterpillars construct large sheets of silk that look like huge
s draped between the twigs of shrubs and trees. The caterpil-
rest in the tents in large groups but leave the tents to feed on
cent vegetation.

and Termite Nests

mounds or termite mounds and nests are other common ex-
les of insect architecture. Obviously they are not something
can collect, but they can be observed, sketched, photographed,
escribed. You can construct ant and termite farms.

Dung Insects and Succession

This project may seem disgusting, but studying dung insects is not as bad as you might think. There are some interesting things to learn about the insects that live in dung and the orderly manner in which certain insect groups follow others as the dung ages. If you live in or near the country where cowpats can be collected, then you are all set to begin.

Cowpats are a good choice because cow manure is not too smelly, especially once the outside of the patty has dried. A dried patty can be studied in the field without disturbing it, or it can be brought indoors and examined more closely.

What You Can Learn

This project will reveal two things. First, you can learn which kinds of insects live in cowpats, and second, you can learn how it takes a succession of insects over time to completely decompose a cowpat. Additionally, observations of life in a cowpat will teach a little bit about insect growth, development, and metamorphosis. Some insects are adapted to feed in the pats when there is lots of moisture, whereas others can only live and feed in the pats after they have dried.

Observing Insects in Cowpats

Select a few cowpats for comparison. Choose one that is very fresh and still moist throughout. Select another that is moist in the center, but dried on the outside. Choose a third that is old and dried throughout. First try to observe or collect the insects that you can see visiting the cowpat or feeding on the outside. Next, pick through each pat using a pair of forceps or probe to discover the insects that are living and feeding there. In fresh and moister pats you will likely find fly larvae or maggots, and other small, soft-bodied insects. In drier and old pats the maggots will be absent and will be replaced by beetle adults and grubs. There will likely be several kinds of each. How many different kinds of insects can you find?

Can you associate the larvae with their adult stages? What makes the insects in fresh pats adapted to the moist environment versus the other insects that thrive in dried pats? These and other questions will result from observing and dissecting cowpats for their insect inhabitants. Are all the insects there to feed on the cow manure, or is it possible that some are there to feed on other insects?

Rearing Insects from Cowpats

If you place a cage over a pat in the field or bring some indoors and keep them covered, you may also have some luck in rearing adult insects. It may be interesting to discover what the maggots and grubs will turn into. You may have seen some of these insects as adults on the outside of pats when you first collected the pats. Over time, the eggs that they laid will hatch and eventually yield the next generation of adults.

Additional Studies

There is one other thing to look for when in the field observing or collecting cowpats. Many cowpat insects will burrow in the moist soil beneath a cowpat. Do not forget to dig a little beneath the pats before you conclude that all the different types of insects have been found.

This project can be more elaborate if you like. You can carefully age cowpats and place screens over them to prevent insects from invading them after a certain time. In this fashion, you can study the nature of insect succession by determining which insects lay eggs in various ages of cowpats. Through a process of elimination you can narrow the list of insects adapted for fresh versus old pats and map the pattern of insect succession in cow manure. Another question to ponder is, how long would a cowpat take to decompose if there were no insects living and feeding there? Can you imagine what the earth would look like without dung-feeding insects? Now that's something really disgusting!

project 6.4
Collecting Galls: Nature's Presents

Plant galls are unusual growths that occur on various plants and plant parts, including leaves, stems, flowers, and fruit. Many are caused by insects that have laid eggs inside the plant. After the egg hatches, the young insect begins to feed, stimulating the plant to form a tissue growth or gall around it. Some people think of galls like plant cancers, but the gall grows in a controlled way and does not usually harm a plant except for the local cosmetic injury. Many insects cause galls, including tiny stingless wasps, midges, caterpillars, aphids, and so on.

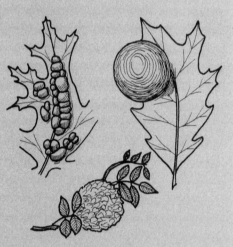

Insect galls of different shapes and sizes are found on various plant parts.

Looking for Galls

Some plants, like oaks and willows, have many kinds of galls that are often conspicuous. On oaks, they are called oak apples, because they are large and round, like fruit on the tree. Some galls are simple swellings of stems or bumps on leaves. Others have interesting shapes and designs. The actual shape of a gall depends on the kind of insect causing it— each kind of gall maker creates its own unique gall. A fun project is to collect as many different galls as you can. Try to name the plant on which they are found, describe the gall type (i.e., leaf gall, stem gall), and see if you can determine what caused it. The best time to look for galls is in the spring or summer when plants are in their active growing phase. Determining the gall former is

Do Bees Sneeze?

tricky, and this is where you might want to dissect or cut into the gall or try to rear the galls and see what insect(s) emerges from them.

Dissecting Galls

To dissect a gall, simply shave off thin slices with a single-edged razor blade or scalpel until you reveal the gall former. The gall former will likely be an insect larva or other immature form. Identifying immature insects can be quite a challenge, so if you have the time and patience you may not want to cut into the gall but set it aside and try to rear the insect(s) from it.

Rearing Gall Insects

To rear an insect gall, place the gall in a dry jar with a screened lid to allow ventilation but prevent tiny insects from escaping. Keep the jar at room temperature and wait to see if anything emerges. If the galls you collect are fresh and do not have holes in them, then there is still a chance something will hatch. Holes in a gall indicate exits for insects that have emerged and departed, or are entryways for other insects that have preyed upon the gall former(s). Timing is everything. To be successful in rearing gall insects you have to collect them when they are nearing their metamorphosis to the adult stage. Don't give up if nothing emerges soon. Some gall insects may overwinter and hatch the following spring. Placing a net cage around the gall in nature is another way to capture hatching gall insects.

Gall-insect biology is a special field of study, so you may want to consult the library for helpful literature.

The willow cone gall, commonly found on wild willows, resembles a pinecone.

Experimenting with Caddisfly Architects

Caddisflies are interesting aquatic insects, many of which are famous for the shelters (called caddises) they construct of sand, pebbles, leaves, and sticks. The shelters are cases constructed by the larval stage and serve as camouflage and protection. The larva wears its protective case to conceal all but the front of its body. Case-making caddisflies are common inhabitants in streams, lakes,

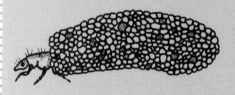

or ponds and can be seen creeping on the bottom or found under or amid submerged objects.

This project allows you to observe caddisfly larvae construct their cases and to experiment with different building materials to see how the choice of material influences the type of case that is constructed. All caddisflies prefer certain building materials and construct cases of a consistent style. For example, some caddisflies are called snail-case makers because they make cases of sand grains that resemble a helical snail shell. Others, called square-case builders, use small sticks to build cases that look like miniature log cabins that are square in cross section. Others may prefer to make cases with leaves or with a combination of materials. There are many interesting styles of cases among the different types of caddisfly construction.

Building Natural Cases

The first step in this project might be to collect as many different kinds of caddisflies and cases as you can. In some areas, there may be diverse types, whereas in other locales there may be only one or a few common caddisflies. Availability will determine the nature of your project. Whether you have one or several types of caddisflies, experiment with their case-building behavior. Use an aquarium that contains the natural materials (leaves, twigs, sand, pebbles) found where your caddisflies live, and begin the experiment by removing a caddisfly from its case. They can be pulled out of their cases if you pull and coax them gently, or you may carefully dismantle or cut the case open to expose the larva. Place the naked and caseless larva in the aquarium among the raw building materials and observe how it finds, gathers, and puts together the stuff it needs for a new case. The caddisfly uses sticky silk to glue its case together—this can be observed as well.

Building Modified Natural Cases
A second experiment involves case construction in the absence of the preferred case-making materials. For example, if you have caddisflies that live in leaf cases, remove the cases and place the naked larva in an aquarium without leaf material but with ample choices of other natural materials. Will the leaf-case maker use sticks, pebbles, or sand in the absence of leaves to build a case? If it does build a case of other materials, is the case design still the same, or has it been drastically altered?

Building Artificial Cases
A third experiment can be conducted to test the caddisfly's ability to build cases of unnatural materials. Use your imagination and provide bits of cardboard, glass, metal, or other combinations of artificial materials. Will the caddisfly use unnatural objects, and how bizarre will their architectural designs become?

Constructing an Insect Aquarium

Many people have aquariums for fish, but how many people have insect aquariums? They are easily constructed and can be populated with insects for interesting observations and enjoyment. They take no more care than a regular aquarium and may in fact get by with far less maintenance. Here are some tips for creating your own insect aquarium.

Materials Needed

Any glass or plastic tank or aquarium can be used. The size is a personal choice, but a 10-gallon aquarium is reasonable. It may be useful to have an air pump and filter as you would in a fish aquarium, but even this is optional depending upon the type of aquatic insect environment that you are trying to duplicate. The easiest environment to mimic in a glass tank is a pond. The water of a pond is essentially still and not as highly oxygenated as a fast-moving stream.

Getting Started

To re-create a pond and its insect life, visit a pond or small lake in your area and observe its general characteristics. What kind of bottom does it have (sandy, muddy, rocky)? Are there aquatic plants (algae, rooted plants)? Is the water fresh or somewhat stagnant? What insects do you see on the surface, in the water, or hiding beneath submerged objects or among vegetation? Collect as many types as you can and store them temporarily in a large container of natural pond water.

Collect enough of the natural substrate (sand, mud, rocks) to cover your aquarium floor to a depth of about two inches, and collect the greatest variety of plants that you think your tank will support. Gather enough of the water to fill the aquarium that you are constructing. Bring the insects and items from their habitat back to your aquarium as soon as possible.

Cover the aquarium floor with your natural substrate and fill the aquarium with the pond water. Add a diversity of plants to provide shelter and enhance the overall appearance. Do not add so many that there is little open water or space, but include enough to create some dense shelters. You can add some sticks or small stones to enhance the appearance and mimic the natural environment. Now add the insects! Just pour them in and leave the aquarium undisturbed for about 24 hours. This will allow suspended particles to settle and the water to clear. It will also allow the insects to seek hiding places and to get accustomed to their new environment.

Discovering and Observing Aquatic Insects

If you have no idea about the numbers and kinds of insects that have been collected and introduced into the aquarium, don't worry. Sometimes it is more fun and interesting to have a real grab bag of creatures and rediscover them as they reveal themselves in the tank. Some will be active swimmers, easily seen as they move throughout the water. Others will cling to the plants and objects placed in the tank. Some may be surface dwellers, and others may be burrowers in the sand or mud. The greater the diversity of insects, the greater the diversity in habits, and the greater the opportunities to learn from observing behaviors.

An important behavior to observe is feeding behavior. You will discover that over time the aquarium will be dominated by a few large or predaceous insects. The smaller species, plant feeders, and scavengers will be eaten by the predaceous types. The aquarium environment will go from a busy and crowded place to a simpler habitat where only the top predators remain. This is when you will want to replenish the tank with fresh insects.

Depending upon the time of year that you have made your collection, you may observe metamorphosis and the emergence of some adult forms from the aquatic immature stages. Emerging mayflies, mosquitoes, caddisflies, and others may appear.

If you know your insects you may want to "stock" the tank with certain types to study certain behaviors. The immature dragonfly has a special jet propulsion that you can observe, and both it and its relative the damselfly have a most unusual lower lip that they use to capture prey. Caddisflies can be observed making cases. Beetles are very visible and active and serve as good examples of insects with special swimming legs. Various insects have special breathing mechanisms: mosquitoes use their snorkel, and many beetles and underwater bugs catch bubbles. The water striders are fascinating for their ability to skate on the water surface and capture insect prey.

The best insect aquarium is one that is populated with the many insects that illustrate all of these habits and that results in constant discoveries and surprises.

144

Do Bees Sneeze?

Making Pitfall Traps

A good spring or summer field project and interesting insect-collecting technique is pitfall trapping. Ground-dwelling insects, especially those that actively walk or run on the soil surface, can easily be trapped with a little critical thinking and some creative strategies.

Materials Needed

- A hand trowel or small shovel
- Some cans (one can for each trap made). A soup can is perfect. The inside walls of the cans must be smooth and vertical, not tapered.

How Pitfall Traps Work

The idea behind pitfall trapping and the basis for developing your trapping strategies is as follows. Many ground-dwelling insects roam the soil surface at night in search of food, mates, and habitat. They are often clumsy and will fall into cavities or depressions in the soil. If a can is buried in the right place, unsuspecting ground-traveling insects will fall in and be unable to crawl out. Obviously, a pitfall trap would not be effective against flying insects or creatures that don't live on the ground.

Setting Up Pitfall Traps

Placing cans randomly in the soil will not result in successful trapping, however. Remember that most insects tend to travel along edges of objects so their body presses against or is close to potential cover. Rarely do insects trek across wide open areas. They prefer to maneuver near and around objects. Therefore, try to locate those spots that you think are most likely to be in the middle of busy insect paths. Against the edge of a log, board, or rock would be good. Near water, near the base of vegetation or along natural gullies and ridges are also prime locations.

Before dark, set out as many pitfalls as you like in the best spots you can find. It is very important to bury the can below the soil surface, leaving absolutely no lip or raised obstruction around the open rim. You want the insect to fall into the pit, not have to crawl up and over a lip to drop in. Also, it's a good idea to somehow mark or map your pitfall sites, because finding them the next day is not always easy.

Collecting Trapped Insects

As soon as you can, visit your pitfalls the next morning and see what may have been captured. Ground beetles are likely to be among the most common, but crickets, ants, and other arthropods are likely to be caught too. If you are not successful on the first try, don't give up. Try some new sites. Sometimes a little bait like a dab of moist dog or cat food can increase trap captures.

When finished, always replace the soil in the pits, and restore the site to its original condition. Never litter by leaving the cans!

Do Bees Sneeze?

7 Foods for Insects & Insects as Food

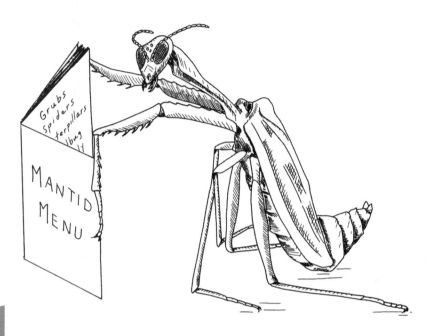

1 What do insects eat?

This is not an easy question to answer because there are so many kinds of insects with so many kinds of food habits. The simple answer is, everything! Some insects eat plants and are called herbivores. Some insects eat other insects and are called carnivores or predators. Some insects eat dead things and are called scavengers. Some insects live close to or on the bodies of other animals and feed on them without killing them and are called parasites. And believe it or not, some insects, once they are full-grown adults, have no mouths and don't eat at all!

Stephen, 2nd grade
Linford Elementary School
Laramie, Wyoming

2 What do bees eat?

Remember that there are many kinds of bees, such as honey bees, bumble bees, sweat bees, carpenter bees, leafcutting bees, orchid bees, and others. Their food habits may vary, but most bees gather nectar and pollen. The honey bee is a good example. Nectar, the sweet liquid that bees find in flowers, contains sugar, or carbohydrates. They lap it up with their tongues. Pollen, a solid food that they also get from flowers, is rich in protein, and also contains the fats, vitamins, and minerals that bees need for a balanced diet.

> Baby bees, or bee larvae, have a different diet. Young workers are fed a mixture of pollen and honey, called bee bread, for most of their lives. Young queens and male bees, the drones, are fed a very protein-rich substance, called royal jelly, that their nurse bees manufacture for them.

The bees collect the pollen on their hairy bodies and legs and can chew it with their strong jaws. Honey bees do not eat pollen and nectar, however. In the hive, they make honey from the nectar and store large amounts of it in their honeycomb, so that when winter arrives and there is no more nectar to be collected, the honey bee feeds on the honey it has made and saved.

Jamin, combined 3rd and 4th grades
Hutton Elementary School
Spokane, Washington

3 What do butterflies eat?

Butterflies, like bees, feed on nectar; however, they have a different way of collecting it. Butterflies do not have a tongue for lapping up nectar like a bee. Instead, they have a long coiled tube, called a proboscis (pro-boss-is), that siphons nectar from flowers. The strawlike proboscis can be uncoiled to reach deep into a flower when the butterfly is ready to feed, and when it is not feeding

Do Bees Sneeze?

the proboscis is coiled tightly like a spring and tucked in against the head. Because butterflies don't have jaws or teeth to eat solid food, they do not eat pollen. Nectar, and the sugar it provides, provides enough nutrition and energy for what is usually a brief adult life.

Jamin, combined 3rd and 4th grades
Hutton Elementary School
Spokane, Washington

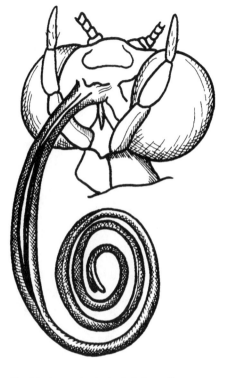

The siphoning mouthparts of a butterfly are like a coiled straw.

4

What do flies eat?

When most people think of flies, they think of the house fly, which I will talk about here, but remember that there are thousands of different kinds of flies with many food habits. Some feed on filth, like dead and decaying animals and plants and animal waste. Others feed on insects; some are scavengers; and some eat the blood of animals and people. Some, like bees, feed on pollen and nectar.

The house fly has a mouth like a sponge, and it prefers to feed on sweet liquids. It also likes to visit nasty things like animal manure, rotting garbage, and dead animals, where it may sponge up smelly liquids to obtain protein. It is very much at home in and around our homes because it will take advantage of any food it might find. It will sponge up liquids,

House fly maggots prefer to live in garbage and animal wastes. A compost heap of household garbage mixed with some dog waste from the yard is an ideal home. There, the maggots feed on the tasty mixture of rotting meat, fruits and vegetables, and manure (tasty to fly maggots, but not to us!).

Food for Insects & Insects as Food

or, for some solid foods, turn them into liquid by spitting up and dissolving them.

Jamin, combined 3rd and 4th grades
Hutton Elementary School
Spokane, Washington

5 Do termites really eat wood?

Yes, and they eat wood products like paper and cardboard, or cow manure, which has a lot of unused cellulose (a chemical in plants and wood that termites like). However, many termites need help to digest their food because their stomachs don't have the chemicals to break the cellulose into small parts that they can use. Therefore, they have tiny one-celled creatures called protozoans and friendly germs, or bacteria, living in their stomach to help them get the nourishment from the wood.

7th grader
Wyoming Center for Teaching and Learning
Laramie, Wyoming

6 Why do cockroaches eat garbage?

Actually cockroaches eat many kinds of food, not just garbage. It is often convenient for them to live off the food scraps and garbage that may lie around our households. Most cockroaches, however, are not household pests and live outdoors, feeding on a variety of plant or animal material. They are mostly scavengers, which means they feed on almost anything they find. Actually, cockroaches often enjoy eating the same things we eat. Would you like to share your peanut butter and jelly sandwich?

Philip, 2nd grade
Linford Elementary School
Laramie, Wyoming

Do Bees Sneeze?

7

Why do ants like sweet foods?

It is true that many ants like sweet foods, but there are other kinds of ants with different food tastes. Those with a "sweet tooth" are attracted to sweets because sweet means sugar, and sugar is an important source of energy. Ants are very busy insects with lots of chores, so they need a

> Ants that do not crave sweets may get their energy and nutrition from other foods like seeds, meat, insects, and fungi (mushrooms). Leaf cutter ants harvest leaves and turn them into fertilizer to grow underground mushroom gardens.

lot of energy to do their work and to survive. Ants can get sweets from flowers and fruit. Many feed on the nectar that plants provide, just as bees do, to get some sugar. Some ants cheat and raid bee hives, stealing honey from the honeycomb. And we all know how ants can invade our homes to find sweet treats in the cupboards and on countertops.

Jason, 5th grade
Starpoint Intermediate
Lockport, New York

8

Do insects eat bigger animals?

There are a lot of insects that eat bigger animals, but not in the same way that a big carnivore, like a lion, eats its prey. The insects that eat bigger animals are scavengers, parasites, and blood-sucking insects. Scavengers are the insects that feed on animals, including big animals, after they are dead. These insects, like fly maggots and beetles, may together eat all of a big animal's flesh and skin, leaving a bare skeleton. These insects have a very important role in nature, because without them we would be buried under dead animal carcasses!

Parasites include such things as lice and fleas, and bots and warbles, which eat bigger animals while living in, on, or near their bodies and sucking blood, chewing skin,

151

Food for Insects & Insects as Food

or burying themselves inside the body. They do not kill the animal, which is called the host, but continue to feed off it for their entire lives.

Blood-sucking insects like mosquitoes and many flies, midges, and gnats feed on bigger animals when they bite and suck blood. They too do not kill the animal, but they rely on bigger animals for their nutrition.

5th grader
Starpoint Intermediate
Lockport, New York

9 How often do insects eat?

This depends on the type of insect, the insect's age or stage of development, and the availability of good food. Immature insects, like caterpillars, maggots, and grubs, seem to eat constantly. Most of their young lives are spent eating in order to gain the nutrition needed to reach adulthood and to reproduce. Cool temperatures, bad weather, poor food or no food, and disturbances may interrupt feeding, but when conditions are right you can bet that these insects live to eat. There will be resting periods during the day or night, and different insects, like people, have their preferred times for dining.

> Some insects eat less, or less often, as adults than they did while growing up. Adult mayflies do not eat at all! They live just long enough to mate and then die. Some blood-sucking insects may need only one blood meal before laying eggs and dying. Some insects, like parasites, have feeding rhythms, which means they feed on a regular schedule. Other insects are not so picky and will feed whenever there is a good opportunity.

Ellie, 5th grade
Starpoint Intermediate
Lockport, New York

Do Bees Sneeze?

10

**How does a praying mantid eat a wasp
without getting stung?**

If a praying mantid is to avoid a wasp's sting it has to be careful, quick, and strong. Mantids are excellent predators and will attack and feed on almost any insect that gets near and that is not too big to handle. With strong front legs that can reach out and grab, and a mouth with strong jaws, the mantid overpowers its prey. Its camouflage allows it to hide from unsuspecting insects and its quickness allows it to capture them in the blink of an eye. A wasp can pose several problems for a mantid. Some may simply be too big and strong for the mantid to catch. If captured, however, the wasp, if it is a female, may sting in self-defense, and this requires the mantid to deliver a quick, disabling or fatal bite. If the mantid is too slow or clumsy it may get stung or injured in the tussle. Insect instincts usually tell the mantid what is a safe and reasonable prey to attack and what should be left alone.

4th grader
Henderson Elementary School
Cheyenne, Wyoming

11

Which bugs, besides mosquitoes, suck blood?

Many other flies (a mosquito is a type of fly) bite animals and suck or lap up blood. Black flies, no-see-ums (a biting midge called that because they are almost too small and quick to see), deer flies, and horse flies are among the most famous. Other insects that eat blood include lice, fleas, certain true bugs like the kissing bug (called that because it likes to bite on the face around the lips) and the bed bug. The true blood-sucking types, like the mosquito, sucking louse, flea, and true bug, have a needlelike mouth for piercing skin and sucking blood.

153

Food for Insects & Insects as Food

Others, like biting flies and midges, cut the skin with a knifelike mouthpart and then lap up the pools of blood with a tongue.

7th grader
Wyoming Center for Teaching and Learning
Laramie, Wyoming

12 Why do bees make honey?

Honey bees make and store honey in their honeycombs for a winter food supply. They usually get plenty of sugar and protein from the nectar and pollen that flowers provide in the spring and summer. They also use the flowers' nectar to make their honey, so that when the flowers and nectar are gone, there will be enough honey in storage to get them through the winter. Only honey bees are able to make honey, and it is because of this special trait that we are able to enjoy honey too.

Julie, 2nd grade
Linford Elementary School
Laramie, Wyoming

13 Why do bugs get eaten by animals?

If it wasn't for bugs, a lot of other animals would not survive. Many animals depend on insects as part of a balanced diet. Some animals eat only insects. Animals that eat insects are called insectivores. Examples of insectivores are many birds, bats, armadillos, anteaters, hedgehogs, moles, and shrews. Even some large animals, like bears, which we usually think of as eating other things, may be insectivorous some of the time. Bugs get eaten because they are nutritious. Insectivores and animals that supplement their diets with insects obtain the vitamins, minerals, sugars, fats, and proteins they need from their insect diet. Insects also get eaten because they are in good supply. Animals can locate insects and often find them in large numbers, making it easy and efficient to feed.

Ashley, combined 3rd and 4th grades
Hutton Elementary School
Spokane, Washington

14

What kinds of bugs are edible, and do they taste good?
Many kinds of insects are eaten by peoples around the world. In fact, almost every major group of insects is enjoyed by some culture. Among the most popular insect foods are grasshoppers and their relatives, termites, beetles (especially the larval or grub stage), caterpillars of butterflies and moths, bee and wasp larvae, ants, and certain water bugs. Most insects are edible, but the favorite ones are those that are large and juicy like caterpillars and grubs or those that can be easily collected and in large amounts, like termites, ants, and bees. The insects that should not be eaten are those that live in filthy and nasty places, such as on animal waste, dead animals, and trash, because of the germs that they may carry. Insects that have bad odors, stinging hairs, harmful bites or stings or are known to taste bad are generally avoided. We learn to recognize many of these kinds by their bright or distinctive warning colors and markings (see question 5, Chapter 2). As far as taste is concerned, insects, like all foods, taste different depending upon type. Some are sweet, some are bitter, some taste nutty, and some may have a slightly fishy taste. Many insects taste a little bit like the foods they eat. If you cook them with salt, butter, and spices, then the insect will be flavored however you like.

6th and 7th graders
Wyoming Center for Teaching and Learning
Laramie, Wyoming

155

Food for Insects & Insects as Food

Finding "Monsters" in Termite Guts!

Many people realize that termites eat wood and wood products, but most will be amazed to discover the monsterous creatures that live inside the termite's stomach and actually help the termite digest its food. These are one-celled organisms called protozoans that live in the termite gut and produce the digestive enzymes. When viewed under a microscope, they look fantastic.

Materials Needed

To discover these stomach monsters you will need some worker termites, a microscope, and a weak saline or salt solution. Collect a few worker termites from rotting logs, wood piles, cow manure or other likely termite homes. The workers are the most numerous of the termite castes and are usually whitish or cream-colored and soft-bodied.

The protozoans that live in termite guts help with digestion.

Finding the "Monsters"

On a glass microscope slide, place a droplet of weak saline (salt) solution. Either cut off the abdomen of a living worker termite and squeeze its contents gently

156

Do Bees Sneeze?

into the droplet, or, if you do not want to kill the insect, then place the tip of its abdomen in the droplet and squeeze gently. Both techniques should result in part of its gut contents, protozoans included, being emptied onto the slide. Cover with a cover slip and observe the fascinating kinds of protozoans. How many kinds can you find? It is fun to draw the different types.

project 7.2
Eating Insects for Dinner

As disgusting as it may sound to some people, insects can be eaten. In fact people of cultures around the world enjoy eating many kinds of insects and gain good nutrition from doing so. Why not eat insects? We eat their closest relatives such as shrimp, crab, and lobster. We eat creatures more lowly than bugs, guts and all, like oysters and snails (escargot). We eat insect products, such as honey. Insects are nutritious, containing vitamins, minerals, protein, and carbohydrates. We actually eat them without knowing it in many of our homegrown or purchased foods. We eat other foods of more questionable origin such as cheeses and sour cream, which are products of bacterial decay. Give an insect a try. There are lots of ways to prepare them and lots of choices among insects to eat.

For information about insects as food and for some recipes, check out the following books and literature:

Dunkel, Florence V., Editor. *The Food Insects Newsletter*. Bozeman, Mont.: Department of Entomology, Montana State University, 59717-0302.

Taylor, Ronald L. *Butterflies in My Stomach: Or, Insects in Human Nutrition*. Santa Barbara, Calif.: Woodbridge Press, 1975.

Taylor, Ronald L., and Barbara J. Carter. *Entertaining with Insects: Or, the Original Guide to Insect Cookery*. Yorba Linda, Calif.: Salutek Publishing, 1992.

Do Bees Sneeze?

Tasting Honey

You may have noticed or perhaps already know that honey comes in different shades, some golden, some pale yellow, some dark like molasses, and some that are almost clear. Each color of honey has its own distinctive flavor. All are naturally sweet, but many have milder or stronger flavors. The colors and flavors depend upon what flower's nectar was predominantly harvested. Sweet-clover honey looks and tastes different from orange-blossom honey. Wild honey, which is made from a combination of flower nectar choices, has a different taste too. Different people have different preferences when it comes to honey. This project is a simple honey-tasting experiment to determine your preferences.

Selecting Honey Varieties

Obtain as many different kinds of honey from the stores as possible. Select them for their different colors or simply refer to the label, which will tell if it is clover honey, apple-blossom honey, or wild honey.

Taking the Honey Taste Test

The best taste test is a "double blind" test. A double blind test means that the person who sets up the test does not know the answer, or in this case does not see the honey label, and the people taking the test can't see the honey labels either. To do this requires one person to secretly code the honey so that only (s)he knows which is which. Before the taste test, show the taste testers each type of honey and ask them which they believe would taste the best. Once they have made their choices, cover the taste testers' eyes. Have them randomly taste each type and describe the flavor. Is it strong or mild, and which is their favorite? After tasting each type, remove the blindfolds and see if the taste testers can guess which taste goes with which color honey.

People who like mild honey will have selected light-colored honey when blind-folded. Persons with a taste for stronger flavors will have selected darker honey when blindfolded. Did their selection of color before being blindfolded match their actual favorite honey? Some honeys may have very similar tastes. You may want to conduct similar taste tests to determine if a person can tell orange-blossom honey from clover honey, and so on.

Do Bees Sneeze?

project 7.4

Creating a Colony
of Insect Vultures

This is not a project for the squeamish, and it will require a space where producing a bad odor will not pose problems.

Insects play a vital role in the decay and decomposition of dead animals and plants. Just as with dung insects, carrion or animal carcasses get recycled due to the feeding by many kinds of insect scavengers. They are the vultures of the insect world. One of the more common carrion feeders is a small beetle called a dermestid or skin beetle. Some dermestids can be pests in the home by feeding on carpets, fabrics, and foodstuffs. Dermestids can destroy an unprotected insect collection. They will eagerly consume dead, dried insects, leaving little piles of insect sawdust where there was once a pinned specimen. They are serious museum pests when allowed to get into mammal skins and mounted birds.

Dermestids for Science

In spite of their pest status in museums, certain kinds of dermestid colonies are actually maintained in museums for a useful purpose. The dermestid larvae and adults are experts at cleaning skeletons. They will feed on the hair, feathers, and tissues of a carcass until it is stripped bare, leaving nothing but a clean, undamaged skeleton. This is very helpful to the museum curator who wishes to mount skeletons or preserve the bones in the museum.

If you wish to observe insect scavengers in action or want to enlist their help in cleaning skeletons for other science projects, then consider establishing your own dermestid colony. You will need a room or container that is large enough to receive animal carcasses or carrion fragments. You will want a room that can be closed securely or a container that can be sealed tightly to prevent escapes and limit the spread of odors.

Starting a Dermestid Colony

To begin a colony you will need to collect some dermestids with some carrion. Roadsides in rural areas are the most likely places to look because of the amount of roadkill. A small mammal that has been dead and already dried out should have a large number of dermestids on, in, or under the carcass. There may be some buried in the shallow soil beneath the carcass. Collect the carcass and beetles in a plastic bag and seal it for the return trip. Use common sense in handling the material to avoid contact with any harmful bacteria. Gloved hands, avoidance of inhalants, and washing afterward are simple precautions.

Establishing the dermestid colony requires the placement of the carcass with its insect guests in the room or container that you have provided for it. The area should be kept dry and at normal room temperature. The dermestids will thrive as long as food lasts. Obviously, to keep a colony going requires replenishing the food supply by collecting new carcasses or by providing bits of old, dried meat and skins.

Feeding Behavior Experiments

You may be surprised to discover that even carrion-feeding insects have likes and dislikes when it comes to food. If you have some different choices of carcasses, try a little experiment by providing equal amounts of each type of food and monitoring the progress the dermestids make in their feeding. In all likelihood they will concentrate on their favorite carcass first and leave the least favorite until last. Experienced museum curators know this and are careful not to give dermestids their favorite carrion when they want them to spend their energies cleaning another type of skeleton.

When you are finished with the dermestid colony, clean your area, bag the remaining beetles and carrion as you did when first collecting them, and return them to their natural setting.

8 Health & Safety

1 Why do bees sting?

Bees sting to protect themselves or to protect their colonies from danger. Only females can sting because the stinger is a customized egg-laying device that only females have. All worker bees are females, and they sting in self-defense and in defense of the colony. The queen bee may use her sting to kill off other queens that try to rule the colony but will rarely sting people.

Ms. Zinda's Challenge Class
Pleasanton Elementary School
Pleasanton, Texas

2 Why do bees die after stinging just once, when wasps can sting over and over again?

Worker honey bees have stingers that are shaped like a fishhook, with a barb at the end. After stinging, the bee

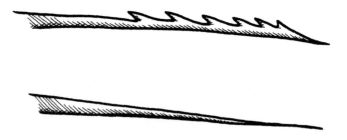

A bee's stinger (top) has barbs while a wasp's stinger (bottom) is needlelike and without barbs.

tries to pull her stinger out but the hooked end or barb remains stuck like an anchor and she rips her guts out attempting to get away. She dies soon afterward. The queen honey bee and wasps have needlelike stingers. The stinger is sharp, smooth, and without a barb, so it can be pulled out quickly and used to sting again without damaging the stinging insect.

4th grader
Wyoming Center for Teaching and Learning
Laramie, Wyoming

3 Do dragonflies have stingers?

Dragonflies do not have stingers and will not sting people. Sometimes people are frightened by them because they may fly close or swoop down at you. Dragonflies can be very jealous of their territories and attempt to chase away other organisms, including people, but they are harmless. There is an insect fable that says dragonflies will fly at people's faces and sew or darn their lips together; hence the names given to them like the

> Some female dragonflies have a device that's something like a stinger that's used for laying eggs. Her ovipositor is like a stinger that can poke into plants and lay eggs inside. These kinds of dragonflies will find plants growing in or near the water for their egg-laying sites.

devil's darners, blue and green darners, and darning needles.

4th-grade class
Henderson Elementary School
Cheyenne, Wyoming

4 Do most bugs bite?

If you mean, "do most insects bite people?" then the answer is no. Most insects are harmless to people and ignore us completely. The ones that do bite us are those that feed on blood (mosquitoes, biting gnats and flies, bed bugs, fleas, and lice) or those that bite to defend themselves. There are some bugs, like the assassin bugs and backswimmers, that can give a painful stinging bite with their beaks if they are disturbed or handled. Sometimes, if our bodies are sweaty, insects like sweat bees will bite because they are attracted by the salty taste. If an insect gets trapped in our clothing and pinched when we put on a sock or a shoe then it might bite because of what we are doing to it. But most insects do not bite us and cannot bite us because of their small size or special kind of mouthparts.

3rd grader
Manor Heights Elementary School
Casper, Wyoming

5 Can ants bite?

Ants have jaws for biting and chewing solid food, so they can certainly bite, but most ants do not bite people. Some ants will bite, and depending upon the type of ant, the bite may be painful, but such bites rarely break the skin. Large harvester ants in the western United States can give a pretty good bite because of their large size and strong jaws. The fire ant of the South will bite and sting. They bite the skin with their jaws to anchor themselves down and then deliver burning stings with

165

Health & Safety

their stingers. Ants usually bite in self-defense or in defense of their colony. Sometimes they might smell or taste something on our skin and take a bite as if we were food, but they won't eat us!

Victoria, 5th grade
Starpoint Intermediate
Lockport, New York

6 Is it true that only female mosquitoes bite?

Yes, it is. The female needs a meal of blood to nourish her eggs so they will hatch. Animal blood has a lot of protein, which is an essential part of her diet and ensures the health of her eggs. She may also eat nectar from flowers and get other kinds of fluids, but blood is essential for reproduction. Therefore, only female mosquitoes bite. The males don't eat blood but suck up plant sap or other natural sweet liquids.

Alex, 7th grade
Wyoming Center for Teaching and Learning
Laramie, Wyoming

7 Do mosquitoes die after they bite?

Eventually she does, but not right away, and not unless you slap her flat before she flies off! After a mosquito bites she may rest, feed again, or lay her eggs. If she is successful, she will bite and feed until she has gotten enough blood to nourish her eggs, and then she will lay her eggs in a pond, lake, puddle, or any other source of standing water, or where water collects after a rain. She may repeat her feeding and egg laying, or she may die shortly after laying her eggs.

Jessica, 5th grade
Starpoint Intermediate
Lockport, New York

166

Do Bees Sneeze?

8 Why do mosquitoe bites make you itch?

We itch from a mosquito bite because we are allergic to the stuff that mosquitoes spit into our bodies when they feed. They are messy feeders and will not just suck our blood but also spit into the wound to keep the blood from clotting in the proboscis. In the same way that our bodies react when we are allergic to pollen, mold, or dust, so too does the body react to an insect bite. There may be some swelling and reddening of the skin, followed by some itching. These are the ways the body acts when it's allergic to something. Some people are more sensitive or allergic to insect bites and stings than others, so the itching can be very mild to very severe.

Mike, 2nd grade
Charles Quentin Elementary School
Lake Zurich, Illinois

9 Can you get AIDS from mosquitoes?

AIDS is a disease that can be transmitted by blood and body fluids, and because mosquitoes go from person to person, feeding on blood, many wonder if the mosquito can spread the disease. There is no evidence that mosquitoes, or any other blood-feeding insect, can transmit AIDS. There are many conditions that have to be just right in order for an insect to pick up, carry, and transmit disease-causing organisms, like the AIDS virus, bacteria, and one-celled animals. Medical entomologists study insects and test their ability to pick up and pass along germs. So far, insects have failed the tests for their ability to spread AIDS.

Ryan, 5th grade
Starpoint Intermediate
Lockport, New York

10

Do a lot of bugs have poison in them?

Most insects are not poisonous and do not have poison in them. The insects most famous for their ability to make poison are the bees and wasps. They have venom- or poison-producing organs and a sting for injecting their enemies or prey. The black widow spider, which is not an insect but an insect relative, is one of the most poisonous creatures in the United States (see question 14, Chapter 9).

Some insects may be poisonous because of the foods they eat, rather than from the poisons their bodies make. The milkweed caterpillar, which turns into the monarch butterfly, is a good example. The caterpillar feeds on milkweed plants, which have a milky-white, poisonous sap in the stems and leaves. This sap tastes bad to most plant-feeding animals and protects the plant from its enemies, but not from the caterpillar. The milkweed caterpillar feasts on the plant and stores the poison in its own body, protecting itself from the birds and animals that eat caterpillars. If something ate a milkweed caterpillar, it would quickly discover its very bitter taste and it might get a very bad upset stomach and throw up. Even after the caterpillar turns into a monarch butterfly, it has the milkweed's poison in the body so it remains protected by a bad taste and nasty side effects.

Maria, 5th grade
Starpoint Intermediate
Lockport, New York

11

What is the deadliest insect in the world?

If you mean, "what insect has the deadliest bite or sting?," then the answer would be the bee or wasp. Every year more people in the United States die from beestings than from rattlesnake bites. This is because we encounter bees much more often than we encounter rattlesnakes, and some people are highly allergic to beestings. If you

Do Bees Sneeze?

have a severe allergy to beestings, then they can be deadly. Fortunately for most people, the beesting may be painful, but it is not deadly.

If, when we say "deadly," we are talking about deadly diseases that insects can spread, then the answer would be the mosquito. Mosquitoes can carry and spread many kinds of diseases, and some of these are deadly. Malaria is a disease spread by mosquitoes, and it kills more people in the world than any other insect-transmitted disease. We are fortunate in the United States because many of the most serious insect-spread diseases have been wiped out or controlled.

> Another deadly, insect-transmitted disease almost wiped out all of Europe during the Middle Ages. The bubonic plague, also known as the black death, was spread by fleas and rats. This disease still exists today but is much better controlled. The nursery rhyme, "Ring around the rosey, pocket full of poseys, ashes, ashes, we all fall down," is really a rhyme about the bubonic plague.

Ms. Zinda's Challenge Class
Pleasanton Elementary School
Pleasanton, Texas

12

How many various diseases can humans get from bugs?
More than 25 major diseases may be carried and spread to people by insects, including such things as malaria, yellow fever, sleeping sickness, dysentery, typhoid fever, bubonic plague, and cholera. There are still others that may be spread by insect relatives, such as Lyme disease and tick fever from ticks.

7th grader
Wyoming Center for Teaching and Learning
Laramie, Wyoming

13

Do insects get colds and die?
Insects do not catch colds as we do, but they can get sick from other kinds of viruses and suffer from certain

169

Health & Safety

diseases and die from their illnesses. Some insects get sick after being attacked by certain kinds of fungi, germs, or bacteria. Sick insects act like sick people. They become somewhat sluggish or slow moving, they lose their appetites, and they just don't appear as healthy. Their color may begin to change or pale. Scientists have learned a lot about the diseases that insects can get and have learned how to use some insect diseases to combat pest insects. For instance, some of the modern pesticides that are sprayed on crops to protect them from plant-eating insects are actually packaged insect germs. Certain fungi and bacteria are being used to control agricultural pests in this way, and mosquitoes and other insect pests that attack people and animals are being controlled by insect diseases. Unfortunately, insect diseases often kill beneficial insects too, so we must be careful in using these and other kinds of pesticides.

2nd grader
Connor Consolidated School
Caribou, Maine

14 Do beetles smell like anything when they die?

When an animal dies it will begin to stink after a while because of the bacteria and other things that help nature's decay or recycling process. I suppose that even beetles smell after they die, but they are usually too small for us to notice any bad odors. If there were lots of beetles dying in one area and their bodies piled up, then we could probably detect their smell. In an insect collection, you can smell the odors of dead beetles and other insects as they dry after being pinned and put in a box. The odor is not strong or long lasting.

Daniel, 5th grade
Starpoint Intermediate
Lockport, New York

170

Do Bees Sneeze?

project 8.1

Good Bugs and Bad Bugs and All Bugs in Between

This is an easy and revealing indoor project that requires no live insects or materials other than a few books or other sources of information on insects. It is based on the belief held by many people that most insects are bad, "yucky," or harmful creatures. Put this belief to the test by generating the biggest list of insects that you can. Use the encyclopedia, the computer, books and literature about insects, or any other resource you have that gives insect names. A group of students will be able to think of quite a few insects without any aids. Don't worry about classification or putting certain kinds of insects together; simply brainstorm the largest roll call of insects that you can.

After you have named as many insects as you can or created a list whose length you like, go back and ask these questions about each insect: Is it bad? (Is it really a pest? Does it harm plants, animals, or people?) Is it good? (Does it play a useful role in nature [i.e., pollinate flowers, help recycle wastes, feed on pests, provide useful products]?) Is it neither good nor bad, but doesn't really affect our lives?

How many insects on the list are truly bad? Good? In between? If you carefully consider these questions for each insect, you will discover that very few are bad. Most are good or, at the very least, in between. Careful consideration of insects in this way will help us remember the valuable role they play in nature.

Health & Safety

9 Insect Relatives

What are ticks?

Ticks are arachnids (ah-rack-nids) that can be found living as parasites on other animals. This means they live for at least part of their lives on the body of an animal called their host. Host animals for ticks may be wildlife, like deer, reptiles, and birds, and also include livestock, pets, and people. Ticks suck blood from their host. They are small and have two body parts, eight legs that reach out to cling to the body, no antennae, and tiny mouths that they bury in the skin when they are ready to eat. Ticks hatch from eggs in the spring and then look for an animal to attack. If you are hiking along a trail or are in the woods where ticks are waiting, they will quietly climb on and seek a nice place to settle down and begin to feed. If not noticed they will suck until they get swollen with blood. When full, they drop from the body and eggs are deposited to repeat the life cycle.

Victoria, 5th grade
Starpoint Intermediate
Lockport, New York

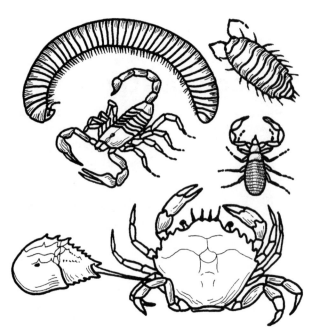

Some representative arthropods—left to right, top: millipede, sow bug; middle: scorpion, pseudoscorpion; bottom: horseshoe crab, crab

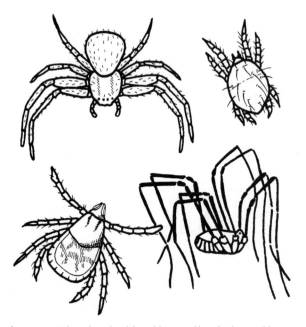

Some representative arthropods—left to right, top: spider, mite; bottom: tick, daddy longlegs

2 Are ticks poisonous?

No, ticks do not have a poison, but like blood-sucking insects, they may carry some germs and a tick bite can make you sick or result in some serious diseases. Some of the sicknesses that come from tick bites are Lyme disease in the eastern United States and Rocky Mountain spotted fever in the Rocky Mountain states, the Midwest, and the eastern United States.

Mike, 2nd grade
Charles Quentin Elementary School
Lake Zurich, Illinois

3 Can ticks smell?

Ticks can smell the breath of nearby animals, and they can smell the perfume of their mates. The carbon dioxide (CO_2) that animals exhale can be detected by nearby ticks. A hungry tick smells CO_2 with special organs on its front feet, and it gets very excited as the odor gets stronger. The tick trys to quickly attach to the animal for a place to live and suck blood. If a tick were unable to smell CO_2 it would not be able to survive. Ticks also find their mates by sense of smell. A tick gives off a strong odor or perfume to attract its mate. If ticks couldn't smell their favorite perfume, they would be unable to locate mates.

Doug, 5th grade
Starpoint Intermediate
Lockport, New York

4 What do mites do in pets' ears?

The mites that you might find in your pet's ears are parasites, similar to ticks (see question 1). They dig into the skin and feed, causing itching and scratching, which often causes the area to get infected. Mites resemble

175

Insect Relatives

tiny little spiders and often are not noticed until you get a whole bunch of them in a single spot. That's why it is important to keep your pet's ears clean and to inspect them now and then for mites. It is better to catch them before they cause severe itching and infection.

Chelsea, 5th grade
Starpoint Intermediate
Lockport, New York

5 Can scorpions be deadly?

Scorpions are arachnids that have two pincerlike claws in front and a long tail with a stinger on the rear. To sting prey or defend themselves from enemies, they can whip their tails quickly and deliver a stinging poison. There are some scorpions whose stings could be deadly to people, but fortunately the most poisonous scorpions do not live in the United States. There is one kind in our country, believed to live only in

Scorpions are not aggressive creatures, usually hiding during the day and coming out at night to hunt. Trouble occurs when people are careless about reaching under objects where scorpions can hide or accidentally finding a scorpion in their shoes or bed. If disturbed, the scorpion will sting.

Arizona, that has a sting that can kill. However, just as with beestings, there are some people who have highly allergic reactions to such poisons—a sting from any scorpion can be risky for them. A scorpion sting can hurt a lot and cause some reddening and swelling where the stinger went in, but fortunately the effects of the sting don't last a long time.

Adrienne, combined 3rd and 4th grades
Hutton Elementary School
Spokane, Washington

Do Bees Sneeze?

6

Do centipedes hunt?

Centipedes are a type of animal called a chilopod. They are active predators and therefore excellent hunters. They have a long, flattened body with many segments that allow them to sneak and crawl under tight places, such as beneath tree bark, under rocks, in soil, and in debris. They have many legs, with two on each body part, and these enable them to run rapidly after prey or away from disturbance. They feed on insects and other small creatures. When they find and capture their prey they use strong fangs to stab, poison, and suck their victims dry. Most centipedes are harmless to people, but there are some large species and some in tropical parts of the world that have dangerous bites.

Patrick, combined 3rd and 4th grades
Hutton Elementary School
Spokane, Washington

7

How many legs does the longest millipede have?

The largest millipede in the United States is about 100 millimeters long, or nearly 4 inches (Borror, Triplehorn, and Johnson 1989, 141). It has 50 pairs of legs (100 in all), and that's why many kids call them "hundred leggers." There are some other millipedes with only 26 total legs. Millipedes have more legs than centipedes, and the legs are packed more closely together, so when a millipede moves it crawls with its legs moving in slow, wavelike patterns. They creep along. Centipedes run faster, with fewer, well-spaced legs.

Danielle, 5th grade
Starpoint Intermediate
Lockport, New York

177

Insect Relatives

8

Why do spiders have eight legs?

Spiders, being arachnids and not true insects, have eight legs instead of six and two body parts instead of three. Their eight legs are all attached to the first body part called the cephalothorax (pronounced seph-ah-low-thor-axe). Eight legs allow the spider to walk in a steady and stable fashion and also to make webs or nests of silk. Having so many legs helps the spider overpower its prey.

2nd grader
Linford Elementary School
Laramie, Wyoming

9

Do some spiders have six legs?

If you see a spider with six legs it may have lost two of its legs in a fight or an accident. Usually lost legs will grow back when the spider sheds its skin as it grows larger.

Katie, 2nd grade
Linford Elementary School
Laramie, Wyoming

10

Why do spiders bite?

Spiders bite in order to feed or to defend themselves. They have special kinds of biting fangs called chelicerae (ka-lis-ah-ree) that stab their prey, squirt poison into the body, and then spit into the body to dissolve tissues and suck the food dry. If you hurt a spider or disturb it, the spider may bite in defense.

Brad, 5th grade
Starpoint Intermediate
Lockport, New York

11

Do spiders really come out at night to bite you?

Many spiders rest during the day and come out at night to feed, but these same spiders do not come out to bite you. You might see them dangling down from your ceiling and by accident they may get on you. Sometimes a sleeping person is bitten by a harmless little house spider simply because (s)he rolled over in their sleep and got in the spider's way. Spiders are not usually aggressive toward people, so we need not worry about them hunting us in our sleep or chasing us around the room at night to take a big bite. The brown recluse spider, however, often bites people in their sleep, and its bite is dangerous.

Jessica, 5th grade
Starpoint Intermediate
Lockport, New York

12

Are all spiders poisonous or harmful?

All spiders have poison glands that make poison for paralyzing their prey. The poison can also help the spider in its own defense. Even though all spiders are poisonous, most are not harmful to people. The poison of most spiders is not strong enough to hurt us, nor is the bite of most spiders big enough to hurt.

Spiders are actually very helpful rather than harmful. They play a very important role in the balance of nature. They feed on millions of insects, helping to keep their numbers from exploding. Spiders are also important as food for other creatures, so they are an important part of nature's food web.

Valerie, combined 3rd and 4th grades
Hutton Elementary School
Spokane, Washington

179

Insect Relatives

13

What will happen if you swallow a poisonous spider?
Perhaps you have heard the song, "There was an old lady who swallowed a fly," and it goes on to say, "there was an old lady who swallowed a spider, it tickled and wiggled, and jiggled inside her." If you swallowed a spider it would not wiggle and jiggle very long because it would quickly die in your stomach. It might tickle on the way down, though. The poison contained in a spider's body would not be dangerous to you if the spider was swallowed. It would be dangerous, though, if a spider like the black widow was going down your throat because its bite along the way could be a killer!

Valerie, combined 3rd and 4th grades
Hutton Elementary School
Spokane, Washington

14

Can black widows be deadly?
Black widows, which are medium-size, smooth, and shiny black spiders with a red hourglass shape on the belly or underside of the abdomen, use a poison or venom like other spiders to attack and feed on their prey. Their poison is especially strong and can be very dangerous, even to people. A strong poison not only helps them paralyze their prey, but it also gives them a very effective defense against their own natural enemies.

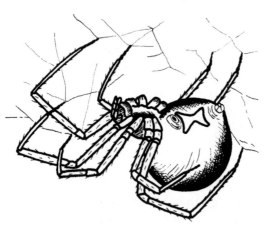

The female black widow spider

The black widow venom attacks our nervous system and causes terrible pain throughout the body. Some highly allergic people may die from a single bite. That

Do Bees Sneeze?

is why it is important to see a doctor if you are ever bitten by a black widow. A bite by a black widow doesn't mean you are definitely going to die, but it is certainly painful and dangerous enough to require immediate medical attention. The black widow is one of only two really dangerous spiders that live in the United States.

Adrienne, combined 3rd and 4th grades
Hutton Elementary School
Spokane, Washington

15 Why are black widows called by that name?

They have the name black widow because the female is black and she may kill and eat her mate after mating is over. By killing her mate she becomes a widow. Some males may escape, but not unless they move away from her and the web quietly, on spider tiptoes, so as not to alert her to the movement. Any little movement or jiggling of the web will cause her to attack and feed on him just as she would on an insect that may get trapped in her web. The good news is that the nourishment she receives by eating her husband helps her eggs to grow, which give rise to many baby black widows. This is recycling at its best!

Brad, 5th grade
Starpoint Intermediate
Lockport, New York

16 How many babies does a spider have?

Spiders usually lay their eggs in little sacs made of silk, and there may be several hundreds of eggs in a sac. Some female spiders make just one egg sac, while others may build several egg sacs, so the number of babies can be very different for different kinds of spiders. It is not unusual for a mother to have hundreds of babies at a time.

Jessica, 5th grade
Starpoint Intermediate
Lockport, New York

Insect Relatives

17

Why do spiders make a web?

Not all spiders make webs, but those that do may make nests with silk webs and they may make webs to trap their food. Among the most famous and best web spinners are the orb weavers. These spiders, like the beautiful golden garden spider, make large silk webs with very intricate or fancy designs. The webs are attached between twigs and other objects in places where flying insects may be common. A spider can make a web every day by tearing down the old one and replacing it with a brand-new one. Once the web is built, the spider will hide or sit quietly with feet touching the web's silk strands, waiting to feel if an insect touches it. When an insect is trapped, the spider quickly paralyzes it with its poison and may then eat it or save it for later. Not all webs are as neat as the orb weavers. Some are messy looking and some are big, flat sheets of silk.

Many spiders let out long strings of web as miniature tripping devices so they can tell when something has crossed their path and may be near enough to catch. The trip strings may tangle and trap the insect prey.

Some spiders make silk webs and use them like nets to catch their food. After making its net the spider will remain alert for insects and throw the net over any unsuspecting victim that gets too close. Some spiders, like trap-door spiders, have a nest in the ground, and their tunnel and trap door are lined with the web. Funnel spiders have a funnel-shaped web and nest in which they trap prey.

Tarin, 5th grade
Starpoint Intermediate
Lockport, New York

18

How do spiders build their webs?

Some spiders are master web builders. They have special silk-producing organs in their bodies to make their

Do Bees Sneeze?

silk, and they have special body parts called spinnerets that release the silk to the outside. They can carefully measure and shape the web to their exact needs. The web is started when the spider hangs down from a single thread of silk anchored to some object. The spider can then climb back up the thread or onto another object and let out another line in another direction. Sometimes they are aided by the wind to span greater distances with their webs. They go back and forth and all around busily designing the shapes they need. They use their legs as rulers to measure the distances between the silken strands and to mark the places where the silk should cross. A complete web can be made in one morning.

Jacob, 2nd grade
Greenvale Park Elementary School
Northfield, Minnesota

19 Why do spiders have that sticky stuff?

When spiders build their silk webs, some of the silk strands will have sticky, gluelike stuff on them. This helps trap insects and other prey that may hit the web and get tangled. The sticky stuff makes it harder for the spider's victim to get away, and it also keeps larger victims from putting up too much of a fight and hurting the spider.

Brad, 2nd grade
Charles Quentin Elementary School
Lake Zurich, Illinois

20 How can you tell if a spider is male or female?

Female spiders are usually larger than the males because a bigger body is necessary for the production of eggs. If you can't compare sizes, look for some special armlike structures near the front. Spiders have a pair of pedipalps (ped-ee-palps) just behind the fangs and in front of the legs. They may look like legs or antennae, but

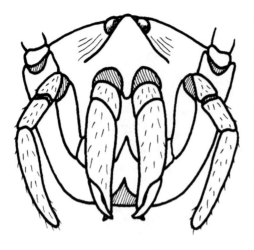

The front pedipalps of spiders are used in mating.

remember a spider can have only eight legs and they never have feelers or antennae. The pedipalps on males are often very large. Some male pedipalps have swollen ends and look like boxing gloves. They use them for courtship and mating. A spider with enlarged pedipalps is a male.

Robert, 5th grade
Starpoint Intermediate
Lockport, New York

21 Can spiders fly?

There is no such thing as a spider with wings, but believe it or not, spiders can be seen flying through the air, sometimes thousands of feet above the ground! How do they do it? They use their silk like a hot air balloon. They can fly through the air by letting out a long trail of silken web that gets caught in the wind and blows the spider to new places. This is called ballooning, because the spiders drift across the sky like a hot air balloon carried by the wind. Ballooning is how many young spiders find new homes.

Taylor, 2nd grade
Charles Quentin Elementary School
Lake Zurich, Illinois

22 What is the biggest spider in the world?

The largest spiders are the tarantulas, which are long-legged, hairy spiders that look frightening to most people. The world record holder for the largest tarantula is the French Guiana "bird eating spider," with a body $3^1/_2$ inches long and a leg span of 10 inches when

184

Do Bees Sneeze?

fully extended. It weighs almost 2 ounces. The heaviest tarantula comes from Brazil. It weighs almost 3 ounces and has a span of 9 $1/2$ inches. (Perrero and Perrero 1979, 6).

Matt, 3rd grade
Manor Heights Elementary School
Casper, Wyoming

23

What is the smallest spider?
There is a family of spiders with members only a fraction of a millimeter in length. These spiders do not have a common name, which is not surprising, because most people would never notice them. In one species of the family, called *Patu digua,* the male is only 0.37 of a millimeter long; smaller than the size of the period at the end of this sentence.

Victoria, 5th grade
Starpoint Intermediate
Lockport, New York

24

Do spiders blink?
Most spiders have eight eyes, but they do not have eyelids, and therefore can't blink, wink, or close their eyes.

Deby and Nate, ages 11 and 10
Monument, Colorado

25

Is it true that daddy longlegs are poisonous?
No, they are not poisonous. They have some special glands which give off a strong chemical smell that may be toxic or repulsive to small animals and birds, but it is not harmful to people. However, I do not recommend eating a daddy longlegs!

6th grader
Wyoming Center for Teaching and Learning
Laramie, Wyoming

Insect Relatives

26

Do rollie pollies have another name?

The rollie pollie is an insect relative that belongs to a class of animals called Crustacea. Other Crustacea include such things as crabs, lobster, shrimp, crayfish, and barnacles. The rolllie pollies are sometimes called pillbugs, because they can roll up into little pill-like balls. Some people call them sowbugs. Sowbugs are related but can't roll up into a pill.

Megan, 4th grade
Anthony T. Lane Elementary School
Alexandria, Virginia

ders are fascinating creatures, in part because of their preda-
us food habits. All spiders prey on other living things and all
e special fangs, or chelicerae, to eat their meals. But the man-
in which they capture and feed differs. An interesting project
o determine the food preferences of different spiders and to
erve their feeding behaviors. For example, one might com-
e two very different kinds of spiders, the orb weavers and
tarantulas.

tching Orb Weavers

o weavers are those spiders best known for their elaborate webs,
structed in vegetation or between objects where flying insects
likely to get trapped. Find an orb weaver in nature and exam-
its web. Can you see the spider? One of the characteristics
t distinguishes different kinds of spiders is the position of the
treat"—(where they wait for their prey); if the retreats are dif-
ent, the spiders are different kinds. The spider may be obvi-
s, resting in the center of the web, or it may be hiding some-
ere near the web's edge. Can you find any of its prey stuck in
web or already wrapped in silk? What has it been catching
l eating? Experiment by offering the spider certain foods. Any
all insect like a fly, midge, butterfly, or beetle may do. When
insect is thrown into the web, how does the spider respond?
es it attack and eat immediately, does it wait to attack, or does
rap and store the prey for a later meal? Do they recognize and
differently toward potentially dangerous prey, such as wasps
l bees? You may be interested in seeing the spider's reaction to
ding a large insect in its web. A large, powerful grasshopper,
example, may be too much for the spider to handle, and the
der will shake the web violently to dislodge what it can't
rcome.

Watching Tarantulas

Tarantulas are becoming common classroom and household p
and they too have interesting behaviors. Their large size ma
them good candidates for actually observing the action of
mouthparts or chelicerae. How do they locate their prey (a cric
mealworm, or some other small insect) when it is dropped nea
Does the spider use silk "trip wires" to help feel the presenc
an insect, or does it simply use its eight eyes? If your tarantu
in a glass jar or tank, you can watch the chelicerae in action c
the tarantula has made its capture. They may look like they
chewing at first, but if you examine them closely, you will
that the spider repeatedly stabs its prey and spits saliva into
body. It appears to be a messy feeder, but this messy liquid h
soften and digest the solid tissues of its prey, so the spider
suck blood and the dissolved body parts of its prey through
hollow chelicerae.

Do Bees Sneeze?

Suggested Readings

Borror, Donald J., Charles A. Triplehorn, and Norman F. Johnson. *An Introduction to the Study of Insects.* Philadelphia, Penn.: Saunders College Publishing, 1989.

Chapman, R. F. *The Insects: Structure and Function.* Cambridge, Mass.: Harvard University Press, 1982.

Cranshaw, Whitney, and Boris Kondratieff. *Bagging Big Bugs: How to Identify, Collect and Display the Largest and Most Colorful Insects of the Rocky Mountain Region.* Golden, Colo.: Fulcrum Publishing, 1995.

Dunkel, Florence V., ed., *The Food Insects Newsletter.* Bozeman, Mont.: Department of Entomology, Montana State University.

Evans, Howard E. *Insect Biology, a Textbook of Entomology.* Reading, Mass.: Addison-Wesley, 1984.

Kneidel, Sally S. *Creepy Crawlies and the Scientific Method: Over 100 Hands-On Science Experiments for Children.* Golden, Colo.: Fulcrum Publishing, 1993.

Perrero, Laurie, and Louis Perrero. *Tarantulas in Nature and as Pets.* Miami, Flor.: Windward Publishing, 1979.

Taylor, Ronald L. *Butterflies in My Stomach: Or, Insects in Human Nutrition.* Santa Barbara, Calif.: Woodbridge Press, 1975.

Taylor, Ronald L., and Barbara J. Carter. *Entertaining with Insects: Or, the Original Guide to Insect Cookery.* Yorba Linda, Calif.: Salutek Publishing, 1992.

Wigglesworth, V. B. *The Life of Insects.* New York: World Publishing, 1964.

Wilson, Edward O. *The Insect Societies.* Cambridge, Mass.: The Belknap Press of Harvard University Press, 1971.

Do Bees Sneeze?

Index to Insects & Insect Relatives

192

Do Bees Sneeze?

Index to Projects

Do Bees Sneeze?